CURRENT AFRICAN ISSUES 46

African Migration, Global Inequalities, and Human Rights
Connecting the Dots
William Minter

NORDISKA AFRIKAINSTITUTET, UPPSALA 2011

INDEXING TERMS:
Migrations
Migrants
Social Inequality
Human rights
Economic and social development
Case Studies
Africa

The opinions expressed in this volume are those of the author
and do not necessarily reflect the views of the Nordic Africa Institute.

ISSN 0280-2171
ISBN 978-91-7106-692-3
© The author and Nordiska Afrikainstitutet 2011
Production: Byrå4
Print on demand, Lightning Source UK Ltd.

CONTENTS

FOREWORD 5
EXECUTIVE SUMMARY 7
INTRODUCTION 10
FRAMING MIGRATION 12
THE DIVERSITY OF AFRICAN MIGRATION 17
MIGRATION FRAMEWORKS: INTERNATIONAL AND INTERNAL 38
MIGRATION AND GLOBAL INEQUALITIES 42
MIGRATION AND DEVELOPMENT 50
MIGRATION AND HUMAN RIGHTS 59
VARIETIES OF MIGRANTS' RIGHTS ORGANIZING 72
FRAMING ADVOCACY AGENDAS 79
REFERENCES: BOOKS, REPORTS, AND ARTICLES 83
REFERENCES: WEBSITES 89
ANNEX: IMPLICATIONS FOR DEVELOPMENT GOALS AND MEASURES 90

FOREWORD

The era of the so-called Washington consensus of market fundamentalism is long past. The developed countries are mired in structural economic crises, while emerging powers such as China, India and Brazil are advancing their economic presence on the world scene and inspiring new policy debates about the prerequisites for development. And a recent joint study by China's International Poverty Reduction Centre and the Development Assistance Committee of the Organisation for Economic Co-operation and Development (OECD) suggests that "Africa will be the next big emerging region".

The Millennium Development Goals (MDGs) set poverty-reduction targets for the year 2015, but they did not fundamentally break with the ideology of market fundamentalism. Addressing only "poverty", these goals avoided fundamental issues of international inequality and social injustice. However, it is now clear to many people, including many policymakers in both rich and poor countries, that economic growth is meaningless unless it is accompanied by measures to reduce the structural inequalities in societies. The post-MDG agenda must focus on addressing the underlying structures of production, distribution and ownership – and of power – that perpetuate imbalances.

In Africa, that means we need developmental states that have the capacity to advance both economic growth and social justice. We need new politics that empower the poor and values that advance common objectives and ethical principles. We need new institutions that really work on behalf of the marginalised segments of society. There must be incentives to improve productivity growth, jobs and incomes, as well as resources for realising human aspirations and human security.

But in our globalised and globalising world, no country, large or small, can advance its own interests without considering its neighbours, its trading partners, its region and, indeed, the entire global order. Developmental states need a developmental world.

In this essay commissioned by the Nordic Africa Institute, William Minter takes migration as an indicator of the need to move beyond the national dimension. Migration, he argues, should not be seen as a self-contained issue, considered in the destination countries as a problem to be managed or in countries of origin as an adjunct to development. Rather, migration should be understood as a process emerging from the relationships between countries, especially inequalities of power and wealth. New measures beyond the MDGs must include the national level of analysis, but also directly address the imbalances between countries.

One must also focus on the rights of migrants themselves. Bringing together results from areas of research most often considered separately, Minter stresses that fundamental human rights are due both to those who decide to leave their countries and those who decide to stay. The rights of migrants are threatened by anti-migrant sentiment, xenophobia and the criminalisation of migration in places as diverse as Norway, Italy, Libya and South Africa. And the rights of the global majority in developing countries are still threatened by a systematically biased global economic order. Until fundamental inequalities between countries are addressed, the pattern of migration in today's world will continue to evoke the spectre of South Africa's apartheid era, when authorities tried to confine blacks to their "homelands", except when their labour was needed elsewhere.

African development and global development, in short, require more than measures to address growth and poverty. Conflicts over migration are dramatic indicators that "development" must also directly confront morally unacceptable global inequalities.

Professor Fantu Cheru
Research Director
The Nordic Africa Institute

EXECUTIVE SUMMARY

The concerns of destination countries and the framing of migration as a problem have long dominated public debate on international migration, and to a lesser extent, policy analysis and scholarly research. Anti-migrant sentiment, leading to restrictive legislation, official abuses against immigrants, and in extreme cases xenophobic violence, is widespread in countries as diverse as South Africa, Libya, Italy, Switzerland, and the United States. Migrants are widely blamed for crime, for "taking our jobs," and for threatening national identity. Empirical evidence to the contrary has had relatively little impact on public opinion.

At the same time, there has been increasing attention in recent years to the impact of migration on the development of migrants' countries of origin, with emphasis on the potential contributions of remittances, efforts to counter the "brain drain" of skilled professionals, and the role of the diaspora in investment and "co-development."

Migrants' rights organisations, particularly in Western Europe, have taken the lead in highlighting the need for protection against abuses of the human rights of migrants themselves. There is also increasing scholarly attention to the topic, as well as multilateral institutional attention by, for example, the UN's Special Rapporteur on the Rights of Migrants and the European Union Agency for Fundamental Rights. But it is still true that the rights of migrants themselves are most often marginalized in official discussions between migrant-receiving and migrant-sending countries.

In 2009, the UNDP Human Development Report called for "win-win-win" approaches to migration policy that would provide benefits for receiving countries, sending countries, and migrants. Such scenarios will have little chance of success unless steps are also taken to address fundamental issues of global inequality so that both those who stay and those who move have access to fundamental human rights. The growing phenomenon of irregular migration, and more generally of "problem" migration that leads to conflict, does not result only from specific national policies. It also derives from rising inequality within and between nations, combined with the technological changes that make migration a conceivable option for larger and larger numbers. Thus trends in migration do not only point to problems or opportunities for development; they also signal fundamental issues facing both those who move and those who do not.

This essay highlights the relationships between different migration issues and the broader context of global inequalities. It "connects the dots" rather than exploring any one issue in depth. It is intended to stimulate further debate and research that can contribute to re-framing migration not as a technical issue for migration specialists, but as one of the fundamental issues that must be addressed in order to bring about a more just global order.

While African refugees, numbering some 2.8 million at the end of 2009, are prominent in the international image of African migrants, they constitute less than 10% of all African-born migrants living outside their country of birth. The majority of African migrants, like the majority of migrants from other world regions, do not fit the definition of refugees fleeing violence or political persecution; rather, they are seeking to escape economic hardship and find better living conditions. Much of that migration is indeed "forced," but the force involved is that of economic inequality between countries and regions.

This paper first reviews African migration by region and then traces frameworks for understanding migration, particularly the links between migration and global inequalities. This sets the context for exploring the specific issues of migration and development and migration and human rights. The paper concludes with examples of migrants' rights organizing, observations on framing advocacy agendas, and an annex suggesting the implications of migration for expanding development goals and measures.

In North Africa, the majority of migrants go to Europe or the Middle East. In Africa's other regions, most migrants move to countries within the African continent, with smaller proportions moving to Europe, North America, the Middle East, or other regions. In West Africa, the movement is largely within the region, from inland to the coast. In Southern Africa, migrants flow predominantly to South Africa. In Central and East Africa, the flows vary markedly by country, depending on geography and on the history of colonial and linguistic ties.

In considering migration and development, the dominant themes of research and debate have been remittances and the flow of skilled labour (brain drain/gain). There has been more attention in recent years to the broader roles of the diaspora population, but the complexity of diaspora relationships remains one of the major areas that needs further attention.

In practice, protection of the rights of migrants, including both refugees and other migrants, falls far short of that already agreed in international law. Although the 1990 Convention on the Rights of Migrant Workers has been ratified by only 44 states, including no major destination country, multiple international human rights agreements require respect for the rights of all people, regardless of migrant status. The failure to respect these universal human rights, and particularly the rights of irregular migrants, is reinforced by anti-immigrant public opinion, by right-wing political mobilisation, and by the practices of governments in their management of migration systems.

Any effective defence of migrants' human rights will require greater organization by migrants themselves, as well as coalitions with other allies committed to justice and human rights.

As illustration, the essay includes brief mentions of four cases of migration-related activism in different contexts: the Sans-Papiers in France, the Black Alliance for Just Immigration in California, the Congress of South African Trade Unions (COSATU), and the Migrants' Rights Network in the United Kingdom.

A final section lays out summary observations about advocacy related to migrants' rights in destination and transit countries, to immigration "reform" and "managed migration," and to migration and global human development.

An annex proposes possible additions to measures of progress based on the Millennium Development Goals (MDGs), stressing (1) measures of global inequality and inequality between countries involved in migration systems, (2) measures that might make the MDG goal 8 of "partnership" less vague, and (3) measures for countries of origin on policies related to emigration and relationships with their diaspora populations.

INTRODUCTION

People have been on the move throughout human history. The ancestors of all of us adapted to changing climate and diverse conditions within Africa, our common continent of origin. Wars, famine, and other hardships have impelled countless migrations over land and sea. From the 16th through the 19th century, the transatlantic slave trade caused the most brutal of displacements. Today, as the global economy drives global inequality, movement across borders, as well as within countries, has reached unprecedented levels.

Africa is no exception to this trend. Migration intersects with almost every other issue affecting the continent, both creating opportunities and contributing to crises. Highly skilled African professionals are now part of global job markets, notably in health, education, the creative arts, and the staffing of multilateral institutions. Both political refugees and economic migrants go south to South Africa, north to Europe, across the Atlantic, and increasingly to Asia as well. Immigration issues, often with sharply racial overtones, are hotly debated in every part of the world, with African immigrants prominently featured particularly in Europe and in South Africa.

The debate on international migration has traditionally focused on the economic and social issues it poses for destination countries. But, as migration scholar Khalid Koser notes, "there has probably been too much attention paid to the challenges posed by migration for destination countries ... and not enough to those that arise for the migrants themselves, their families, [and] the people and societies they leave behind" (Koser 2007: 12).

Increasingly for Africa, as well as for international migration more generally, attention has focused on topics such as remittances and related links between migration and development, as well as on the traditional issues posed for destination countries. But this new perspective goes only so far. The narrowly focused policy debates rarely address the links between migration and widening inequalities, both between and within nations, as well as the policies that increase these inequalities. Most discussions of migration take national and international inequalities as given, rather than seeing tensions over migration as signals that those inequalities have reached unacceptable levels.

Societies are just beginning to grapple with the biases and fears underlying anti-immigrant actions in places as diverse as Arizona, Italy, or South Africa. Nor has there yet been wide public debate on the changing conceptions of citizenship in a transnational economy or the fundamental concept of human rights due to migrants regardless of their legal status. Only 44 countries have ratified the International Convention on the Protection of the Rights of All Migrant Workers and Members of their Families, and those that have signed do not include South Africa or any major destination country in Europe or North America.

Resolving the immediate issues of migration policy will require new thinking that can reach beyond specialist discussions to change the framework of public policy debate. The aim of this essay is not to present original research on specific migration topics, but rather to connect the dots. It highlights emerging advocacy efforts among African migrant groups and civil society both in Africa and outside the continent, as well as new critical thinking by scholars and policy analysts. While the essay contains references to the research and policy literature,[1] the primary emphasis will be on raising fundamental questions, particularly those related to unequal life chances and unequal rights.

There is inequality within every country. But today's inequalities are overwhelmingly determined by national divisions.[2] In such a world, it should be no surprise that people try to move to get a better deal. The phenomenon is worldwide, and especially pronounced wherever wealth and poverty coexist in close proximity: Africans from around the continent find their way to South Africa, South Asians and Africans find work in the Middle East, Mexicans and Central Americans cross the border to the U.S. Southwest. People risk their lives on small boats from Africa to Europe, or from the Caribbean to Florida.

In South Africa, under apartheid, the authorities tried to confine blacks to their "homelands," except when their labour was needed elsewhere. The system of migrant labour set up to serve the diamond and gold mines of the late 19th century became a comprehensive system for allocating differential political and economic rights. The economy of white South Africa relied on black labour from South Africa's rural areas and surrounding countries, denying political rights and calibrating movement of people to the demands of employers. But even the massive apparatus of the apartheid state failed to stop "excess" population movement, despite repeated deportations of "surplus people" without proper passes.

The systematic inequality in today's world, which condemns millions of people to grinding poverty and untimely death, should be as unacceptable as slavery, colonialism, and apartheid. There are complex policy issues involved, and many obstacles to fundamental change. In this essay I will argue that addressing specific issues, such as xenophobic violence, "brain drain," or the contribution of remittances to development, is insufficient without also rethinking assumptions about the relationship of life chances and rights to nationality as an accident of birth, which, like race, gender, or ethnic group, should not serve as justification for differential treatment.

---

1. See Adepoju (2008) for a comprehensive survey and extensive bibliography on sub-Saharan Africa by a leading expert. For additional references consulted for this essay, most published since 2008, see the list of books, articles, and reports at the end of the paper.
2. See Korzeniewicz and Moran (2009) and Milanovic (2011).

FRAMING MIGRATION

Public debate on international migration, and to a lesser extent policy analysis and scholarly research, tends to be dominated by the concerns of destination countries and by the framing of migration as a problem. Anti-migrant sentiment, leading to restrictive legislation, to official abuses against immigrants, and in extreme cases to xenophobic violence, is widespread in countries as diverse as South Africa, Libya, Italy, Switzerland, and the United States. Migrants are widely blamed for crime, for "taking our jobs," or for threatening national identity—with empirical evidence to the contrary having relatively little impact on public opinion.

> **Note on Terminology**
>
> The term "migrant" is sometimes used to refer only to "migrant workers" and their families, thus excluding those with the international legal status of "refugee" or "asylum seeker." However, it is also, and more commonly, used to refer to all those living outside their country of birth for a sustained period of time, thus including both refugees and others. In this paper, migrant is used in the more general sense.
>
> A refugee is defined for the UN High Commission on Refugees as "someone who, owing to a well-founded fear of being persecuted for reasons of race, religion, nationality, membership of a particular social group or political opinion, is outside the country of his nationality and is unable or, owing to such fear, is unwilling to avail himself of the protection of that country." An asylum seeker is a person seeking refugee status.
>
> Those migrants having documented status in their country of residence are referred to as "regular" or "documented" migrants, while those lacking such status are referred to as "irregular" or "undocumented." The terms "legal" and "illegal" are also in common use, but are generally regarded as pejorative.
>
> The term "forced migrant" is sometimes used as synonymous with "refugee," but not in this paper. As will be noted later in the paper, the conceptual distinction between "forced migration" and "voluntary migration" is inherently ambiguous and hard to define.

Opinion polls show that the most extreme anti-migrant views are rarely in the majority, yet they often set the terms of debate. The World Values Survey, for example, covering more than 50 countries (http://www.worldvaluessurvey.org), shows 11% of respondents calling for prohibiting any immigrants from coming, 38% for setting strict limits on immigration, 39% for allowing immigration as long as jobs are available, and 13% for letting anyone come who wants to.

The World Values Survey also showed wide variations among countries in openness to immigrants. In South Africa, for example, only 16% favoured letting immigrants in if jobs were available, and 6% were for letting anyone come, while 78% supported stricter limits. In Mali, by contrast, 46% favoured letting immigrants in if jobs were available, and 34% supported letting anyone come, with only 20% supporting stricter limits. In the United States, the comparable figures were 37% for admitting immigrants if jobs were available, 7% for letting anyone come, and 57% for stricter limits. In Germany, 43% favoured allowing immigrants in if jobs were available, 7% were for letting anyone come, and 50% were for stricter limits. (For additional data and analysis see Kleemans and Klugman 2009; UNDP 2009: 89-92; and Transatlantic Trends 2010).[3]

The dominant policy response to such attitudes has been to propose better management of immigration by destination countries. This includes, on the one hand, measures to secure borders and expel undocumented or irregular immigrants, and on the other hand, programs to match legal immigration to job needs. Most countries encourage immigration of skilled professionals and provide procedures for assimilation of a manageable fraction of immigrants as citizens. Increasingly these measures have been combined with efforts to engage sending countries in enforcement campaigns and to promote development that might reduce the "push" for emigration.

Countries of origin have also long identified emigration as a problem, especially in terms of the much-discussed "brain drain" of skilled professionals. In recent years, however, there has been a strong push by international agencies and sending countries to stress the benefits of emigration, notably the inflows of financial remittances and the engagement of diaspora professionals and organizations in their home country's development. Unlike the debate on immigration in destination countries, the growing discussion of migration and development in the sending countries has largely been confined to policy analysts and scholars, with only limited impact in the arena of public debate. Only a few countries, notably Cape Verde, Mali, and Morocco in Africa and the Philippines in Asia, have made policies regarding emigrants major components of their development strategies.

In all countries, however—both sending and receiving—the focus is much more on what's good for the country and its native-born residents than on the rights and interests of the migrants themselves. Migrants tend to be framed either as victims or as villains, a story apparently more enticing than the mun-

---

3. A survey by Transatlantic Trends (2010) compared the United States, Canada, the United Kingdom, France, Germany, Italy, the Netherlands, and Spain, showing significant variations on different questions related to immigration. In one question, the survey asked whether there are "too many" immigrants, "a lot but not too many," or "not many." When given no information on the actual percentage, those saying "too many" ranged with 59% in the UK to 17% in Canada. However, when estimates of the actual percentage were provided before asking the question, those saying "too many" dropped to under 50% in every case (from 46% in the UK to 13% in Canada).

dane but realistic narrative in which migrants make rational decisions, migrate without incident, and succeed in improving conditions for themselves and their families. Many migrants are indeed desperate, fleeing political violence or economic destitution in their countries of origin. That desperation is reflected in the deaths at sea in the Atlantic Ocean, the Caribbean, the Mediterranean, and the Gulf of Aden, and in the burning desert along the U.S.-Mexican border. And some migrants are involved in criminal activity, including human trafficking and drug smuggling. But these non-representative images, which dominate the policy debate, are not the norm. They reinforce scare scenarios of migrant "invasions" and disregard the agency and initiative of migrants themselves.

They also reinforce what scholars de Haas (2009) and Bakewell (2009) have recently termed the "sedentarist" bias, namely the assumption that human mobility is somehow unnatural rather a normal feature of human development, and that people in general would be better off "staying in their place" (Bakewell 2008). Such a bias prevails despite contrary trends such as, for example, the more frequent celebration of immigration and multiculturalism in immigrant destinations such as the United States, Canada, and Australia, in "world cities" such as London, and in many European countries as well. African diaspora professionals are increasingly prominent in the leadership of international organizations, in world music and sports, and in the medical profession, as well as in a wide variety of other contexts in North America, Europe, and elsewhere. But their prominence co-exists with stereotypes still widely applied to others of the same national origins.

In this paper I argue, following the lead of the UNDP's 2009 Human Development Report, that it is essential to find a new frame for thinking about migration, one that takes mobility as normal. Such a framework should prioritize the agency and rights of migrants themselves while also paying attention to the interests of destination and origin countries. But migration should not be considered in isolation. The "win-win-win" scenario envisaged by the Human Development Report will have little chance of success unless steps are taken to address fundamental issues of global inequality, so that both those who stay and those who move have access to fundamental human rights. The scale of irregular migration, and more generally of "problem" migration that leads to conflict, does not result only from specific national policies. It also derives from rising inequality within and between nations, combined with the technological changes that make migration a conceivable option for larger and larger numbers. Thus trends in migration do not only point to problems or opportunities for development; they also signal fundamental issues facing both those who move and those who do not.

Previewing the Argument

1. Migration, both inside a country and internationally, has long been among the normal options for human beings who seek to achieve a better life or escape unacceptable hardships. While most people prefer to stay close to their place of birth, others are willing or feel compelled to leave. As the globalization of ideas, trade, finance, and communications continues to grow, the proportion of people who want to move, including across national boundaries, is likely to continue to grow as well.

2. It is impossible to say exactly how much of this migration should be regarded as "forced." Some people clearly are forced to flee by violence or persecution. In other cases, desperate economic conditions allow people no effective choice but to leave their places of birth for other regions or cities in their home countries or in other countries.

3. The extraordinarily high and growing inequality between countries, reproduced by an increasingly integrated global economy, results in levels of international migration that are unsustainable for destination countries, conducive to human rights abuses against migrants, and potentially damaging to countries of origin, which lose valuable human resources.

4. In Africa, as is well known, various conflicts have produced refugees and internally displaced persons. At the same time, it should be recognized that there are structurally embedded migration systems driven by economic disparities between African countries and between Africa and the rest of the world. These migration pathways have drawn people from Africa to Europe, North America, and the Middle East; from West, Central, and East Africa to North and South Africa; and from one locale to another within African regions.

5. Despite anti-immigrant sentiment and a push to restrict immigration in destination countries, stopping or significantly slowing migration is not a realistic option. Nor would that be consistent with the rights of human beings to seek better lives for themselves regardless of national boundaries.

6. The UNDP has outlined "win-win-win" options for migration policies that might simultaneously benefit destination countries, origin countries, and migrants themselves. These offer significant potential for reducing the negative effects of migration and enhancing its benefits for all concerned. But vested interests, prejudice, and imbalances of power stand as formidable obstacles to the enactment and implementation of such policies.

7. Enhancing the contribution of migration to development in countries of origin requires attention not only to the familiar topic of brain drain, but also to inequality between countries involved in a migration system and to the need for ensuring mutually beneficial ties between countries of origin and their diasporas.

(continued)

> **Previewing the Argument** (continued)
>
> 8. Protecting the interests of migrants requires a rights-based approach that defends the applicability of fundamental human rights to migrants and also protects and expands the right to migrate. This in turn requires both initiative from migrant organizations and alliances with other forces seeking social justice in the countries of destination.
>
> 9. Such efforts will be insufficient, however, unless steps are taken to address the fundamental transnational inequalities that underlie the pressure for large-scale migration. A sustainable solution for migration is only possible in a world in which people have effective rights and real choices, whether they stay within their country of birth or decide to move to another country.

Before sketching the possible shape of such a framework and its relevance to Africa, it is important to summarize the empirical diversity of African migration. Migrants from African countries are diverse in terms of their origins, their destinations, their legal status, and their education and skills.

THE DIVERSITY OF AFRICAN MIGRATION

In the year 2000, the baseline for the most comprehensive comparative survey of international migrants worldwide, there were approximately 183 million people living outside their country of birth or 3% of total world population.[4] They included approximately 24.6 million Africans, a little more than 13% and roughly in line with the percentage of Africans in the world population. The largest number of international migrants were born in Asia (about 63 million) or in Europe (about 55 million), with migration rates ranging from a low of 1.1% for Northern America to a high of 7.3% for Europe (driven, in part, by the breakup of the former Soviet Union into multiple countries). Africa's migration rate, 2.9% of people born on the African continent and now living outside their country of birth, was only slightly under the world average.

In the last half century, the total number of international migrants has expanded significantly, from 77 million in 1960 to 195 million in 2005 and an estimated 214 million in 2010. The share of migrants in the world population also grew, but only modestly, from 2.6% in 1960 to 3.1% in 2010.

Table 1 shows the distribution of African migrants by region, again using estimates from the year 2000. Among approximately 7.4 million migrants from North Africa, 57% were in Western Europe, 26% in the Middle East (outside Africa), and only 10% in other African countries. For the 17.2 million migrants born in Sub-Saharan Africa, the pattern was the reverse: 72% were in other African countries, 16% in Western Europe, and less than 12% elsewhere in the world, including 5.5% in Northern America and 4% in the Middle East.

The diverse migration streams, by country, can be seen in more detail in Tables 2 and 3. The patterns are shaped by historical and linguistic ties as well as geographical proximity. For example, a large percentage of Liberian migrants and a moderately high percentage of other migrants from English-speaking African countries go to Northern America (Canada and the United States).

Table 4 shows the size of the African-born population in 26 countries, also in the year 2000, from data compiled by the Organisation for Economic Co-operation and Development (OECD).[5] Although it does not include Germany, which does not track immigrants by place of birth, or important non-OECD

---

4. These numbers, like all statistics connected to migration, should be considered very approximate "best estimates," given the many caveats on data collection and compilation. There are large disparities between data compiled from different sources. See Batalova (2008) for a review of the major data sources. The figures in this paragraph are calculated from Table A in UNDP (2009). Note also that almost all statistical sources do not taken into account second-generation immigrants born in the destination country to immigrant parents. The "immigrant community" is therefore in almost all cases substantially larger than the number of foreign-born or the number of foreign citizens resident in a country.
5. Note that these numbers vary somewhat from those in Table 1, an indication of the possible range of error in both sets of statistics.

TABLE 1. WORLDWIDE DISTRIBUTION OF AFRICAN IMMIGRANTS, 2000

Origins	From North Africa	From North Africa (%)	From Sub-Saharan Africa	From Sub-Saharan Africa (%)	From Africa	From Africa (%)
Emigrants by Region Outside Africa	7,388,904	100	17,247,343	100	24,636,247	100
Oceania	39,596	0.5	183,499	1.1	223,095	0.9
Asia	133,711	1.8	305,303	1.8	439,014	1.8
Northern America	296,621	4.0	942,125	5.5	1,238,746	5.0
Canada	91,994	1.2	215,511	1.2	307,505	1.2
United States	204,627	2.8	726,614	4.2	931,241	3.8
Latin America & Caribbean	18,114	0.2	41,135	0.2	59,249	0.2
W. Europe	4,210,368	57.0	2,776,713	16.1	6,987,081	28.4
Belgium	142,093	1.9	103,229	0.6	245,322	1.0
France	2,481,672	33.6	567,049	3.3	3,048,721	12.4
Germany	617,500	8.4	469,497	2.7	1,086,997	4.4
Great Britain	71,715	1.0	770,531	4.5	842,246	3.4
Italy	248,682	3.4	133,600	0.8	382,282	1.6
Netherlands	173,549	2.3	101,519	0.6	275,068	1.1
Portugal	1,709	0.0	348,115	2.0	349,824	1.4
Spain	346,383	4.7	73,327	0.4	419,710	1.7
Sweden	12,747	0.2	49,592	0.3	62,339	0.3
Switzerland	37,961	0.5	49,342	0.3	87,303	0.4
E. Europe & Central Asia	150,529	2.0	199,932	1.2	350,461	1.4
Middle East	1,941,897	26.3	653,959	3.8	2,595,856	10.5
Total Outside Africa	6,657,125	90.1	4,797,363	27.8	11,454,488	46.5
Africa						
North Africa	304,228	4.1	142,942	0.8	447,170	1.8
Sub-Saharan Africa	427,551	5.8	12,307,038	71.4	12,734,589	51.7
Total in Africa	731,779	9.9	12,449,980	72.2	13,181,759	53.5

Source: Global Migrant Origin Database, Version 4
http://www.migrationdrc.org/research/typesofmigration/global_migrant_origin_database.html

destinations such as the Middle Eastern states, it shows most countries outside the African continent in which African immigrants form significant population blocks. The largest number are in France (some 2.7 million), the United States (838,000), United Kingdom (763,000), Italy (407,000), Spain (372,000), Portugal (332,000), Canada (278,000), Belgium (232,000), the Netherlands (216,000), and Australia (166,000). The countries with the largest proportion of African-born residents are France (with almost 6%), Portugal (almost 4%), and Belgium (almost 3%). Others with over 1% African-born include the Netherlands, Spain, the United Kingdom, Canada, Australia, Switzerland, New Zealand, and Luxembourg.

In 2000, as can be seen in Table 4, none of the Nordic countries had more than 1% of the population African-born. By 2010, however, according to na-

TABLE 2. INTERNATIONAL EMIGRANTS BY AREA OF RESIDENCE

	Continent of Residence, 2000–2002 (% of Total Emigrant Stocks)					
	Africa	Asia	Europe	Latin America and the Caribbean	Northern America	Oceania
Algeria	9.5	6.8	81.6	0.2	1.8	0.1
Angola	65.8	3.8	28.6	0.8	1.0	0.0
Benin	91.6	3.1	4.6	0.2	0.5	0.0
Botswana	60.3	2.7	21.3	0.2	10.8	4.7
Burkina Faso	94.0	3.0	2.4	0.2	0.3	0.0
Burundi	90.8	3.2	4.6	0.2	1.1	0.0
Cameroon	48.9	3.2	38.8	0.2	8.9	0.1
Cape Verde	33.8	3.0	49.1	0.2	14.0	0.0
Central African Republic	84.1	2.1	13.0	0.2	0.6	0.1
Chad	90.7	5.5	3.1	0.2	0.5	0.0
Comoros	42.0	4.8	52.4	0.2	0.6	0.0
Congo	80.1	2.1	16.5	0.2	1.1	0.0
Congo (Democratic Republic of the)	79.7	2.6	15.3	0.2	2.2	0.0
Côte d'Ivoire	47.7	3.1	43.4	0.2	5.6	0.1
Djibouti	41.7	5.0	48	0.2	4.7	0.5
Egypt	10.5	70.5	9.7	0.3	7.4	1.6
Equatorial Guinea	77.9	3.0	18.3	0.2	0.6	0.0
Eritrea	78.2	11.5	5.6	0.2	4.3	0.3
Ethiopia	8.6	37.5	21.4	0.2	30.7	1.5
Gabon	69.9	2.1	26.1	0.2	1.7	0.0
Gambia	44.7	2.9	39.7	0.2	12.4	0.1
Ghana	74.8	3.4	12.2	0.2	9.1	0.2
Guinea	90.3	3.0	5.1	0.2	1.4	0.0
Guinea-Bissau	65.0	2.8	31.3	0.2	0.6	0.0
Kenya	41.5	4.2	37.9	0.2	14.4	1.8
Lesotho	93.5	2.3	2.8	0.1	1.1	0.2
Liberia	34.9	4.4	11.5	0.2	48.8	0.2
Libyan Arab Jamahiriya	16.3	39.8	26.7	0.4	14.7	2.0
Madagascar	28.2	3.0	65.8	0.5	2.4	0.1
Malawi	83.7	2.5	11.6	0.2	1.7	0.4
Mali	91.1	3.1	5.1	0.2	0.5	0.0
Mauritania	75.9	4.5	17.1	0.2	2.3	0.0
Mauritius	32.8	2.6	49.7	0.2	4.9	9.8
Morocco	9.1	13.2	74.5	0.2	2.8	0.1
Mozambique	83.8	2.5	12.8	0.3	0.6	0.1
Namibia	77.8	2.5	11.3	0.2	5.4	2.7
Niger	93.3	3.0	3.0	0.2	0.5	0.0
Nigeria	62.3	4.4	18.1	0.2	14.8	0.2
Rwanda	85.2	3.2	9.1	0.2	2.3	0.0
Sao Tome and Principe	27.2	3.0	69.0	0.2	0.6	0.0
Senegal	55.7	3.0	38.1	0.2	2.9	0.0
Seychelles	39.7	2.7	32.1	0.2	10.4	14.9
Sierra Leone	40.9	3.0	31.5	0.2	24.0	0.5
Somalia	50.8	9.6	27.5	0.2	10.8	1.0
South Africa	38.6	3.3	30.5	0.3	13.8	13.5
Sudan	42.9	45.9	5.7	0.2	4.6	0.8
Swaziland	72.5	3.2	14.9	0.2	7.1	2.1
Tanzania (United Republic of)	67.5	2.8	17.4	0.2	11.4	0.7
Togo	83.8	2.7	11.3	0.2	2.0	0.0
Tunisia	9.3	9.9	78.3	0.2	2.3	0.1
Uganda	37.5	3.7	43.9	0.2	13.9	0.9
Zambia	78.3	2.9	13.2	0.2	3.8	1.6
Zimbabwe	61.8	3.0	24.1	0.2	5.7	5.1
Africa	52.6	12.5	28.9	0.2	4.9	0.9
Asia	1.7	54.7	24.5	0.5	16.4	2.2
Europe	2.5	16.0	59	2.5	15.4	4.6
Latin America and the Caribbean	1.1	5.1	10.3	13.4	69.8	0.3
Northern America	2.2	14.7	23.6	21.0	34.9	3.7
Oceania	1.4	8.7	20.1	0.6	22.5	46.7
Sub-Saharan Africa	72.7	4.1	16.6	0.2	5.2	1.1
World	**9.1**	**28.2**	**33.4**	**3.4**	**23**	**2.9**

Source: UNDP (2009, Table B)

TABLE 3. EMIGRANTS BY COUNTRY

Origin Countries	Total Africa	North Africa	Sub-Saharan Africa	Africa	Outside Africa	Ratio of Emigrants Outside Africa to Emigrants in Africa
North Africa	**7,388,904**	**304,228**	**427,551**	**731,779**	**6,657,125**	**9.1**
Morocco	2,546,519	101,578	135,249	236,827	2,309,692	9.8
Tunisia	596,189	25,191	31,112	56,303	539,886	9.6
Algeria	2,033,811	81,861	115,130	196,991	1,836,820	9.3
Egypt	2,135,610	88,611	140,277	228,888	1,906,722	8.3
Libyan Arab Jamahiriya	76,775	6,987	5,783	12,770	64,005	5.0
Southern Africa	**3,241,202**	**5,832**	**2,170,211**	**2,176,043**	**1,065,159**	**0.5**
Angola	856,132	1,200	577,962	579,162	276,970	0.5
Botswana	16,359	30	9,982	10,012	6,347	0.6
Lesotho	50,341	70	47,571	47,641	2,700	0.1
Malawi	148,473	241	125,676	125,917	22,556	0.2
Mozambique	836,108	1,172	709,393	710,565	125,543	0.2
Namibia	24,066	696	18,278	18,974	5,092	0.3
South Africa	770,741	1,497	301,267	302,764	467,977	1.5
Swaziland	11,620	23	8,516	8,539	3,081	0.4
Zambia	243,301	386	193,475	193,861	49,440	0.3
Zimbabwe	284,061	517	178,091	178,608	105,453	0.6
East Africa	**3,295,277**	**111,365**	**1,488,289**	**1,599,654**	**1,695,623**	**1.1**
Comoros	47,532	2,749	17,563	20,312	27,220	1.3
Djibouti	16,704	1,136	5,955	7,091	9,613	1.4
Eritrea	558,714	24,998	419,375	444,373	114,341	0.3
Ethiopia	279,532	1,429	23,200	24,629	254,903	10.3
Kenya	444,006	950	188,389	189,339	254,667	1.3
Madagascar	147,938	302	42,197	42,499	105,439	2.5
Mauritius	172,481	265	57,080	57,345	115,136	2.0
Mayotte	300	0	277	277	23	0.1
Reunion	169	0	10	10	159	15.9
Seychelles	16,575	50	6,625	6,675	9,900	1.5
Somalia	529,494	25,396	248,324	273,720	255,774	0.9
Sudan	631,806	52,992	222,434	275,426	356,380	1.3
Tanzania, United Republic of	282,819	677	193,119	193,796	89,023	0.5
Uganda	167,207	421	63,741	64,162	103,045	1.6
Central Africa	**2,723,761**	**5,249**	**2,217,231**	**2,222,480**	**501,281**	**0.2**
Burundi	381,653	681	352,493	353,174	28,479	0.1
Cameroon	167,293	489	82,745	83,234	84,059	1.0
Central African Republic	108,493	244	91,937	92,181	16,312	0.2
Chad	300,322	958	274,249	275,207	25,115	0.1
Congo	542,170	819	437,643	438,462	103,708	0.2
Congo, the Democratic Republic of the	809,617	1,302	653,113	654,415	155,202	0.2
Equatorial Guinea	93,634	158	73,997	74,155	19,479	0.3
Gabon	57,210	88	40,280	40,368	16,842	0.4
Rwanda	235,751	470	204,120	204,590	31,161	0.2
Saint Helena	5,284	8	510	518	4,766	9.2
Sao Tome and Principe	22,334	32	6,144	6,176	16,158	2.6
West Africa	**7,987,103**	**20,496**	**6,431,307**	**6,451,803**	**1,535,300**	**0.2**
Benin	566,358	936	526,795	527,731	38,627	0.1
Burkina Faso	1,325,509	2,113	1,266,101	1,268,214	57,295	0.0
Cape Verde	196,276	289	67,147	67,436	128,840	1.9
Cote d'Ivoire	173,562	628	83,575	84,203	89,359	1.1
Gambia	50,853	136	22,959	23,095	27,758	1.2
Ghana	938,608	1,823	715,039	716,862	221,746	0.3
Guinea	573,607	1,174	525,787	526,961	46,646	0.1
Guinea-Bissau	126,181	301	83,082	83,383	42,798	0.5
Liberia	83,159	201	29,694	29,895	53,264	1.8
Mali	1,551,131	2,786	1,435,119	1,437,905	113,226	0.1
Mauritania	115,074	4,710	83,985	88,695	26,379	0.3
Niger	488,210	907	462,422	463,329	24,881	0.1
Nigeria	1,023,394	2,576	646,264	648,840	374,554	0.6
Senegal	471,373	1,366	265,720	267,086	204,287	0.8
Sierra Leone	92,822	211	38,410	38,621	54,201	1.4
Togo	210,986	339	179,208	179,547	31,439	0.2
Sub-Saharan Africa	**17,247,343**	**142,942**	**12,307,038**	**12,449,980**	**4,797,363**	**0.4**
Africa	**24,636,247**	**447,170**	**12,734,589**	**13,181,759**	**11,454,488**	**0.9**

TABLE 4. AFRICAN AND FOREIGN-BORN POPULATION IN SELECTED OECD COUNTRIES

Country of Residence	Born in Africa	Total Foreign-Born	All Countries of Birth	African-Born as % of Foreign-Born	African-Born as % of Total Population	Foreign-Born as % of Total Population
OECD - Total	6,677,536	67,883,912	783,682,530	9.84	0.85	8.66
France	2,745,341	5,600,198	48,068,377	49.02	5.71	11.65
United States	838,233	31,389,926	217,165,205	2.67	0.39	14.45
United Kingdom	762,575	4,503,466	47,684,484	16.93	1.60	9.44
Italy	407,470	2,020,934	48,892,559	20.16	0.83	4.13
Spain	372,120	1,914,920	34,848,140	19.43	1.07	5.50
Portugal	332,393	585,932	8,699,515	56.73	3.82	6.74
Canada	277,500	5,355,210	23,900,785	5.18	1.16	22.41
Belgium	232,434	1,019,302	8,491,529	22.80	2.74	12.00
Netherlands	215,958	1,419,946	12,733,410	15.21	1.70	11.15
Australia	166,094	3,860,215	14,856,774	4.30	1.12	25.98
Switzerland	61,628	1,454,185	6,043,350	4.24	1.02	24.06
Sweden	56,470	933,830	6,463,865	6.05	0.87	14.45
Greece	50,957	999,911	9,273,198	5.10	0.55	10.78
New Zealand	30,021	624,093	2,889,633	4.81	1.04	21.60
Norway	28,932	305,923	3,666,921	9.46	0.79	8.34
Denmark	26,026	319,301	4,358,618	8.15	0.60	7.33
Austria	22,397	923,692	6,679,444	2.42	0.34	13.83
Ireland	21,525	332,988	3,034,605	6.46	0.71	10.97
Finland	8,075	112,430	4,244,575	7.18	0.19	2.65
Luxembourg	5,326	129,761	356,342	4.10	1.49	36.41
Japan	5,069	1,142,367	108,224,783	0.44	0.00	1.06
Turkey	4,349	1,130,552	47,583,832	0.38	0.01	2.38
Poland	1,998	737,733	31,288,416	0.27	0.01	2.36
Czech Republic	1,787	436,966	8,571,715	0.41	0.02	5.10
Hungary	1,775	275,494	8,503,379	0.64	0.02	3.24
Mexico	809	241,462	62,842,638	0.34	0.00	0.38
Slovak Republic	274	113,175	4,316,438	0.24	0.01	2.62

Source: Database on Immigrants in OECD Countries (DIOC) http://stats.oecd.org
Data extracted on Oct. 13. 2010 from OECD Stats. The data comes from 2000 census or equivalent. Note that Germany is not included as census reports citizenship rather than place of birth.

tional statistics[6], the African-born population had reached 1.05% in Norway and 1.23% in Sweden. It had increased from 0.19% to 0.33% in Finland over the decade, while in Denmark the percentage dropped slightly from 0.6% to 0.58%. Overall, in 2010, there were 215,000 African-born recorded in these four Nordic countries, for slightly less than 0.9% of the population.

The numbers for the Nordic countries reflect several factors with distinct effects. The region's countries are not traditional immigration countries (except from within the Nordic region), sharing neither colonial, linguistic, nor geographical closeness with Africa or other immigration regions. But all except Denmark rank high on the Migration Integration Policy Index rating policies towards immigrants (www.mipex.eu). Particularly relevant for immigration from Africa is a relatively open policy toward asylum-seekers. This accounts

---

6. Available on-line at the relevant national statistics agencies: www.statistikbanken.dk, www.stat.fi, www.ssb.no, and www.scb.se.

for the fact that the largest national group among African-born residents in the Nordic countries is from Somalia, with 72,000, about a third of the total. Other relatively large groups are from Ethiopia (19,800), Morocco (18,300, part of the wider expansion of Moroccan economic migration in Europe), and Eritrea (15,300).

While exploration of this theme for specific countries goes beyond the scope of this paper, it is notable that anti-immigrant political movements on the European continent, already significant in Denmark and Norway before 2000, have also recently gained ground in Sweden and in Finland.

Despite the fact that the majority of African immigrants in the Nordic countries are refugees rather than work-seekers, the issues raised increasingly resemble those elsewhere in Europe.

International migrants, including those from Africa, are diverse not only in terms of their origins and destinations, but also in many other ways. Undocumented or irregular migrants (often pejoratively labelled "illegal") are those who have no documentation or inadequate documentation of their legal right to be in the destination country. They include those who enter countries without papers, those who overstay their visas, those who stay on after being refused asylum, and, in the case of legal residents, those who are working without authorization to do so. Statistics for these groups of migrants are rarely available. Estimates for irregular migration as a proportion of the total in developed countries range from 5% to 15%; as much as one-third of migration in developing countries could be irregular (Sabates-Wheeler 2009: 4; IOM 2010: 120). But these data are highly uncertain. In some cases, such as South Africa, there is a common perception that the proportion of "irregular" migrants may be several times higher than indicated by official figures. But the scholarly consensus is that the data for South Africa are insufficient to provide reliable estimates, and that popular estimates are wildly exaggerated (Polzer 2010a; Landau and Segatti 2009).

A much more clearly defined category is that of migrants with refugee status, since this is incorporated into international law, and monitored by both national and international agencies. According to statistics from the United Nations High Commissioner for Refugees (UNHCR), at the end of 2009 there were 15.2 million refugees worldwide, including 4.8 million Palestinians and 10.4 million people under UNHCR responsibility. The largest number were from Asia (6.4 million), and the next largest from Africa (2.8 million). African refugees were therefore less than 10% of the total number of African international migrants (24.6 million in 2000, and probably some 29 million by 2009). Internally displaced people were some 15.6 million worldwide, with 6.5 million in Africa, more than twice the number of African refugees.

Finally, migrants differ significantly by skill level. Table 5 shows the distribution of migrants to OECD countries by education level for African countries and for world regions. Among African migrants to OECD countries, 44.6% have less than upper secondary education, 28.6% have upper secondary education, and 24.5% have advanced education, a distribution not that different from world averages. Among migrants to OECD countries from Sub-Saharan Africa, only 31.9% have less than upper secondary education, while 31.6% have upper secondary education and 33.1% have advanced education. The greatest contrast between African migrants and those from elsewhere in the world is the "tertiary education ratio," that is, the proportion of those with advanced education living outside their countries. While the world average is 3.7%, it is 9.1% for the African continent, and 12.2% for sub-Saharan Africa.

The character of migration flows differs considerably from one African region to another, as well as by country within region. The following sections provide brief summaries and illustrative country cases for Africa's five regions, with particular attention to more general issues in the analysis of African migration.

North Africa

As befits its intermediate position, both geographically and in economic rankings, North Africa is exceptional among African regions. The majority of its emigrants go not to other African countries but to Europe and to the Middle East (in 2000, 57% and 26% respectively). And increasingly, North African countries not only send migrants but also serve as destination and transit countries.

As can be seen in Table 2, Morocco, Algeria, and Tunisia each send over 70% of their emigrants to Europe; Egypt sends over 70% to Asia, while Libyan emigrants go to Asia (40%) and Europe (27%).[7] The scale and duration of the migratory flows from North Africa to countries outside Africa (almost 7 million in 2000, and some 8 million by 2005) show that these migration streams are almost certainly long-term structural features of the regional economies, part of an established migration system with effects on both origin and destination countries.

Among the regional migration streams, that from the Maghreb (Morocco, Algeria, and Tunisia) to France is the most solidly established. During World War I, France recruited migrants from the Maghreb for its army, industry, and mines. Recruitment continued during World War II, the postwar period, and the postcolonial period as well, although the national distribution changed, particularly due to the war for independence in Algeria. During that war, France

---

7. The single best source for description and analysis of migration from and to North Africa is the work of Hein de Haas. See particularly de Haas (2007) for migration from North Africa, and de Haas (2006) for trans-Saharan migration to and through North Africa. A wide variety of other publications are available through his website (http://www.heindehaas.com).

TABLE 5: EDUCATION AND EMPLOYMENT OF INTERNATIONAL MIGRANTS IN OECD COUNTRIES (AGED 15 YEARS AND ABOVE).

	Stock of International Migrants in OECD Countries (Aged 15 or above) (thousands)	Educational Attainment Levels of International Migrants			Tertiary Emigration Rate
		Low Less than Upper Secondary	Medium Upper Secondary	High Tertiary	
		(% of all migrants aged 15 and above)			
Algeria	1313,3	55,4	27,8	16,4	15,4
Angola	196.2	52.9	26.5	19.5	..
Benin	14.4	25.8	30.5	42.2	11.3
Botswana	4.1	12.3	46.3	37.1	4.2
Burkina Faso	8.3	46.9	22.6	28.5	..
Burundi	10.6	24.3	28.7	38.0	..
Cameroon	58.5	23.3	32.3	41.9	12.5
Cape Verde	87.9	73.7	19.1	5.9	..
Central African Republic	9.8	33.4	33.1	32.7	9.1
Chad	5.8	22.7	33.1	42.2	..
Comoros	17.6	63.6	25.6	10.7	..
Congo	68.7	27.1	34.2	34.9	25.7
Congo (Democratic Republic of the)	100.7	25.0	32.5	35.5	9.6
Côte d'Ivoire	62.6	38.1	34.2	26.4	..
Djibouti	5.4	34.1	34.7	29.7	..
Egypt	308.7	18.8	30.7	47.3	3.7
Equatorial Guinea	12.1	52.0	25.5	22.4	..
Eritrea	48.0	36.0	39.3	20.7	..
Ethiopia	124.4	24.3	43.6	29.2	..
Gabon	10.8	29.9	33.1	35.9	..
Gambia	20.9	47.9	30.9	16.5	44.6
Ghana	165.6	26.5	38.4	31.3	33.7
Guinea	21.3	49.6	25.4	22.4	..
Guinea-Bissau	30.0	66.3	20.5	12.8	71.5
Kenya	198.1	26.0	32.7	36.9	27.2
Lesotho	0.9	18.3	31.6	45.8	3.8
Liberia	41.0	20.6	44.8	33.5	24.7
Libyan Arab Jamahiriya	64.8	44.3	30.6	23.6	..
Madagascar	76.6	33.3	34.6	31.7	..
Malawi	14.9	32.5	28.5	34.8	15.5
Mali	45.2	68.3	18.7	12.6	14.6
Mauritania	15.2	63.1	19.1	17.2	..
Mauritius	91.4	42.9	27.9	24.4	48.5
Morocco	1505	61.1	23.1	13.9	..
Mozambique	85.7	44.2	28.8	26.4	53.6
Namibia	3.1	15.3	34.8	45.9	..
Niger	4.8	26.6	34.3	37.5	5.8
Nigeria	261	15.5	28.4	53.1	..
Rwanda	14.8	25.4	32.6	34.9	20.8
Sao Tome and Principe	11.6	72.2	16.9	10.7	..
Senegal	133.2	56.6	23.6	19.1	18.6
Seychelles	8.1	42.6	31.5	17.3	..
Sierra Leone	40.2	23.5	37.4	33.7	34.5
Somalia	125.1	44.0	30.6	12.5	..
South Africa	351.7	14.6	34.6	44.8	6.8
Sudan	42.1	23.4	32.9	39.7	4.6
Swaziland	1.8	19.8	32.9	42.9	3.2
Tanzania (United Republic of)	70.2	25.1	30.4	40.7	15.6
Togo	18.4	27.9	34.1	35.8	11.8
Tunisia	427.5	55.5	27.8	15.9	14.3
Uganda	82.1	27.4	29	39	24.2
Zambia	34.9	14.2	34.4	47.9	15.5
Zimbabwe	77.4	14.9	39.9	40.6	9.4

	Stock of International Migrants in OECD Countries (Aged 15 or above) (thousands)	Educational Attainment Levels of International Migrants			Tertiary Emigration Rate
		Low Less than Upper Secondary	Medium Upper Secondary	High Tertiary	
		(% of all migrants aged 15 and above)			
Africa	6555.3	44.6	28.6	24.5	9.3
Asia	17522	33	29.8	34.3	3.6
Europe	27318.1	38.6	35.7	21.6	7
Latin America and the Caribbean	18623	53.8	31.9	13.8	6
Northern America	1923.8	18.8	35.8	42.5	0.7
Oceania	1098.2	26.6	38.7	27.4	4
Sub-Saharan Africa	**2761**	**31.9**	**31.6**	**33.1**	**12.2**
World	75715.9	41	32.7	23.5	3.7

recruited more workers from Morocco. After Algerian independence in 1962, over one million migrants left Algeria for France, including both French colonists and Algerians who had fought on the French side during the war. In the 1960s and early 1970s, in response to European recruitment of "guest workers," migration from the Maghreb continued to grow, extending beyond France to countries such as Germany, Belgium, and the Netherlands.

The second major migration stream in the region, to oil-producing Arab states in the Gulf and to Libya, took off after the 1973 oil crisis. Egypt, which under Nasser had a policy of restricting emigration, opened up the doors under Sadat. This led to the departure of some 2.3 million Egyptians by the mid-1980s, mainly to the oil states of the Gulf. Libya also began to attract emigrants, particularly from Egypt, Morocco, and Tunisia.

While it boosted the economies of the Gulf states, the oil crisis also heralded economic downturn in Europe. European countries turned to more restrictive policies, limiting new immigration and encouraging guest workers to return home. However, the restrictions actually encouraged many Maghrebi migrants to stay permanently, since they feared that if they left Europe they would find it more difficult to return. These settled migrants then brought family members to join them. Similarly, although the 1991 Gulf War led to repatriation of migrants from the Gulf to North Africa, and increased the Gulf states' preference for South Asian immigrants, migrant flows from Egypt to the Gulf nevertheless continued.

In the last two decades, three major developments introduced new currents into the stream of migration from North Africa to Europe. With rising demand for unskilled labour in southern Europe, migration from Africa increased to that region, particularly to Italy and Spain. At the same time, Italy and Spain introduced new visa requirements, ensuring that a rising proportion of that immigration was irregular. In addition, increasing numbers of migrants from West

Africa began reaching North Africa, a flow stimulated by recruitment to Libya. While many stayed in North Africa, others used North Africa as a launching point for reaching Europe. Many succeeded, but some did not: West Africans, as well as North Africans, began to feature regularly in reports of migrants lost at sea in the Mediterranean or in the Atlantic.

As Europe tightened its admission requirements and enforcement measures, it also began to pressure North African and West African states to cooperate in reducing immigration. Libya, where migrants constituted at least 10% of the population by 2000, joined in stepping up deportations, driven both by popular anti-immigrant sentiment and by government policies agreed with Europe.[8] Yet, according to Hein de Haas and other researchers, these measures did not alter the fundamental trends based on the need for labour in Europe and supply of labour available from Africa. They did, however, ensure that a rising proportion of migrants were forced into more risky means to reach their destinations and contribute to a misleading image of "an invasion" of destitute migrants.

Despite the increase in irregular African immigration into Europe and of the proportion of Sub-Saharan African immigrants, that image is misleading. The dominant migration flows from North Africa continued to be North Africans joining the already large North African population in Europe through regular channels. North African migrants in Europe outnumber migrants from Sub-Saharan Africa by more than 50% (see Table 1). West Africans trying to reach Europe illegally through North Africa were only a small fraction compared with West Africans reaching Europe through regular channels on direct flights (de Haas 2008b, 9). And North African countries, far from being only a transit route to Europe, have became destination countries themselves. There are probably more West Africans living in the Maghreb than in Europe (de Haas 2008b: 9). And that, in turn, is a smaller proportion than West African migration within West Africa itself.

West Africa

While the flow of West Africans across the Sahara and on to Europe has been attracting attention, the dominant West African migration streams continue to be those established in the colonial period, which have expanded in volume in recent decades. These are, first of all, migration within the region—from the interior to the coast, from urban to rural areas, and from countries with fewer economic opportunities to those offering jobs in agriculture and industry. Sec-

---

8. The backlash against Sub-Saharan African migrants in Libya began with clashes in 2000, followed by a range of repressive measures, including detentions and deportations. For documentation see reports by Human Rights Watch (http://www.hrw.org/middle-eastn-africa/libya).

ondly, there is the migration of students and professionals to the former colonial powers and increasingly to other developed countries as well.[9]

Within West African countries, an average of 3.2% of residents are immigrants from other countries, and emigrants from each country constitute an average of 2.9% of their respective populations (de Haas 2008b: 21). Of emigrants from West African countries, 61% stay within the region, with 15% going to Europe and 6% to North America. Mobility within the region has been facilitated by the ECOWAS 1979 Protocol Relating to Free Movement of Persons, Residence and Establishment. While this protocol is not yet fully implemented, freedom of movement is substantial. All ECOWAS countries have abolished visa and entry requirements for community nationals for stays of up to 90 days. And nine of the 15 ECOWAS countries, including Ghana, Nigeria, and Senegal, issue ECOWAS passports to their nationals.

Intra-regional mobility has been and still is characterized by a predominantly north-to-south and inland-to-coast movement. The countries with the largest numbers of immigrants (as of the year 2000) were Côte d'Ivoire, Ghana, Nigeria, and Burkina Faso. The largest number of emigrants came from Mali, Burkina Faso, Ghana, Nigeria, and Senegal. Nigeria, Ghana, and Senegal also sent the most West African migrants to Europe and North America. Significantly, however, West African countries sent only small fractions of their populations as migrants to OECD countries (de Haas 2008b: 24). Only Cape Verde has a high rate of emigration to OECD countries, about 23%. Guinea-Bissau has a rate of 2.4%, and five other West African countries (the Gambia, Ghana, Liberia, Senegal, and Sierra Leone) have rates of 1% or more.

Among Sub-Saharan African regions, West Africa has the lowest number of refugees and asylum seekers, only 158,000 compared to 469,000 in Southern Africa, almost 900,000 in East Africa, and almost a million in Central Africa (UNHCR 2010: 26). Despite the return of peace to Liberia, the majority of the refugees in the region are still from that country. If one includes internally displaced people as well as refugees and asylum seekers, however, the 851,000 number in West Africa exceeds the 469,000 in Southern Africa, driven by more than 500,000 internally displaced within Côte d'Ivoire.

Each country in West Africa has its own distinctive migration pattern, shaped primarily by its geographical position and colonial history. While all are both origin and destination countries for migrants, the balance differs widely, from the largest net outflow of 38% in Cape Verde and over 10% in Mali to net inflows over 10% in Côte d'Ivoire, Gabon, and The Gambia. Countries such as Burkina Faso and Ghana have both high inflows and high outflows, but end up

---

9. For convenient summaries of the West African migration system, see Bakewell and de Haas (2007, 9-13) and International Organization of Migration (2010: 140-143). De Haas (2008b) provides a more compehensive overview.

with contrasting balances, a net outflow of 3% in Burkina Faso and a net inflow of 4% in Ghana.[10]

Two countries with contrasting migration patterns, Ghana and Côte d'Ivoire, point to the range of issues raised, many with parallels to other countries on the continent. Ghana illustrates, for example, the importance of internal as well as international migration, and the problem of emigration of skilled workers ("brain drain") even in countries generally regarded as politically stable and economically successful. Côte d'Ivoire, on the other hand, illustrates the interaction of generations of migration with current issues of citizenship and internal political divisions, an issue that also dominates the intertwined histories of countries of the Great Lakes region.

Ghana's international migration includes significant flows of both immigrants and emigrants. Its internal migration is mainly from north to south and from rural areas to urban areas. In 2005, the foreign-born population made up 7.6% of Ghana's resident population, with almost 60% coming from other West African states and the remainder from elsewhere in Africa and from outside the continent. Emigration from Ghana has gone through significant shifts over time. Economic decline led to large-scale emigration to Nigeria in the late 1970s and early 1980s, but this was reversed when as many as 1 million Ghanaians were expelled from Nigeria in 1983 (Anarfi and Kwankye 2003). In the last two decades, Ghanaian emigrants, including many skilled professionals, have created a wide-ranging Ghanaian diaspora, with a significant presence in other English-speaking African countries as well as in North America and Europe.[11] Ghana's tertiary emigration rate (the proportion of university-trained Ghanaians living outside the country) was high at 33.7% (see Table 5).

In West Africa, Côte d'Ivoire ranks the highest in the number of residents born outside the country, and second to The Gambia in the percentage of foreign-born residents. An estimated 2.3 million residents (13.5%) in 2000 were born outside the country; by 2010 the estimate had risen to 2.4 million, while the percentage dropped to 11.2%. If second-generation immigrants are included, the percentage of immigrant population is roughly doubled (some 26% of the total population in 2000).[12]

The system of labour migration to Ivorian plantations and other economic

---

10. De Haas (2008b: 21). These estimates refer to the year 2000. More recent figures from Ghana show closely balanced inflows and outflows, with a very small net outflow (Quartey 2009).
11. The issue of migration of skilled professionals and other issues prominent in Ghana, such as internal child migration from north to south, are explored most comprehensively in a series of studies by the Development Research Centre on Migration, Globalisation & Poverty (http://www.migrationdrc.org).
12. For a clear background account of migration and citizenship issues in Côte d'Ivoire, see Manby (2009: 81-95). See also Conchiglia (2007).

sectors, primarily from Francophone inland states, was well established during the colonial period, and reinforced during the presidency of Félix Houphouët-Boigny, who ruled from independence until his death in 1993. Later presidents, including Laurent Gbagbo, elected in 2000, opportunistically used the concept of *ivoirité* to mobilize anti-immigrant sentiment for electoral advantage. The distinction between immigrants and northerners belonging to the same ethnic groups was often blurred, linking the issue to one of ethnic rivalry. Many residents of immigrant parentage were denied citizenship, while land law was changed to allow only citizens to own land. Acquisition of citizenship was made more difficult, and a 2000 referendum changed the constitution to deny the right to run for office to anyone who lacks full proof of both paternal and maternal Ivorian ancestry. There followed more than a decade of conflict, which was not resolved despite successive peace pacts and an internationally recognized election won by opposition leader Alassane Ouattara. Although Ouattara was installed in power after months of conflict in early 2011, the prospects for national unity remain elusive.

Southern Africa

For more than a century the political economy of Southern Africa has been moulded by a complex pattern of labour migration and political exclusion. The mining economy established in South Africa in the late 19th century relied on labour not only from South Africa's rural areas but also from neighbouring countries. Miners from Lesotho, Mozambique, and other countries formed the majority of the mining work force until the 1970s; they continued to make up some 40% of the total thereafter, despite new preferences given to South African workers. Migrants from the Southern Africa region also worked inside South Africa in agriculture, industry, and the informal sector. But only whites were considered potential permanent immigrants, with African immigrants defined as "foreign natives."[13]

Internally, pass laws defined the rights of South Africa's own Africans. None had political rights, and only some were granted rights of residence in urban and other "white" areas. This system, established in the late 19th century, was systematized and intensified under the "apartheid" label in the period following World War II. The pass laws and forced removals of Africans to rural "homelands" were among the most visible and widely denounced aspects of the apartheid system. The Group Areas Act regulated where those classified as Indians or Coloureds by the apartheid state were allowed to live and do business.

---

13. For a convenient summary, see Crush, Williams, and Peberdy (2005). For more detailed accounts, classic sources include Crush, Jeeves, and Yudelman (1991) and Wilson and Ramphele (1989).

The end of political apartheid in 1994 dismantled racial barriers to residence and to economic and political advance. But South Africa remains one of the most unequal countries in the world, and overall levels of inequality have even increased (Leibbrandt et al. 2010). These internal legacies of apartheid have been widely debated. Until recently, however, the effects of apartheid thinking on regional structures of inequality, reflected in the treatment of regional migrants in South Africa, has not faced similar public scrutiny.[14]

Illegal as well as legal migration to South Africa continued to grow in the post-1994 period, driven both by economic disparities and by the arrival of political refugees. In addition to migrants from the traditional Southern African sending countries, Somalis, Nigerians, and Congolese are among the nationalities prominently represented and visible in urban centres, particularly Johannesburg and Cape Town.

A widespread outbreak of xenophobic violence in May 2008, which led to over 60 deaths, brought new attention to the issue. So has the ongoing drama of migrants from Zimbabwe, roughly estimated as between 1 and 1.5 million, most undocumented, who were granted temporary protection from deportation in 2009 and 2010, but many of whom may face deportation in 2011.[15] There is still much disagreement about the causes of and the remedies for anti-immigrant sentiment in South Africa—even the use of the term xenophobia is contested—and about the potential for further violence. But the evidence shows that hostility to foreigners from other African countries is "pervasive, deep-rooted and structural, cutting across all divides" in South African society (Crush and Ramachandran 2009: 14). As these authors point out, this sentiment is shared by the majority of South Africans of all races and classes, making South African views on immigrants among the most hostile anywhere in the world (see also Kleeman and Klugman 2009: 11). This is despite the fact that the South African Constitution explicitly extends basic human rights to all residents.

Sensationalist media coverage has encouraged misconceptions and stereotypes. Media reports feature images such as a "flood" or "invasion" of migrants. There are no reliable data on the numbers of foreign-born in South Africa, but the total is most likely between 1.6 and 2 million people, or approximately 3% to 4% of the population—hardly an invasion (Polzer 2010a).

Among the most detailed surveys of attitudes was the one done in 2006 by the Southern African Migration Programme (Crush 2008). In that survey,

---

14. Nevertheless, there has been significant research for some time, most notably the extensive work of the Southern African Migration Programme (http://www.queensu.ca/samp), which was founded in 1996.
15. For well-researched summary studies see Polzer (2010a: 2010b), Landau and Segatti (2009), and Crush (2008). Strategy and Tactics (2010) provides both analysis and original research, prominently featuring the response by civil society. Two other prominent works, of less consistent quality, are Neocosmos 2010 and Hassim, Kupe, and Worby 2008.

67% of South African respondents regarded migrants as a criminal threat, and the same proportion said that foreigners consumed resources that should be allocated to South Africans. A majority of respondents had unfavourable impressions of migrants whatever their origin.

Migrants from North America and Europe were regarded more favourably (an average of 22% favourable) than those from African countries, and those from Lesotho, Botswana, and Swaziland more favourably than those from elsewhere in Africa. Angolans, Congolese, Somalis, and Nigerians, as well as Mozambicans and Zimbabweans, were viewed most unfavourably. Thirty-seven percent of respondents favoured a total ban on immigration of foreign nationals, while 38% said there should be strict limits, and 84% said South Africa was letting too many foreign nationals into the country (Crush 2008: 24).

Strong anti-immigrant sentiment makes significant policy reform difficult, but it by no means implies that violence is inevitable. Research by the Forced Migration Studies Programme (Polzer 2010b), considering both the 2008 violence and subsequent case studies in 12 communities, compared areas where violence occurred and where it did not. It concluded that violence against foreign nationals was not more prevalent in locales with the highest rates of unemployment or the highest percentages of foreign residents. Although it did occur in areas with high levels of economic deprivation, male residents, and informal housing, violence was typically triggered by the competition of leaders for local political and economic power, which occurred in areas with weak local governance structures. The implication is that even in the absence of adequate policy at the national level, local governments and civil society coalitions can have an impact on curbing violence.

Despite policy changes in 2002 favouring skilled immigration, the admission of a limited number of refugees, and a temporary amnesty for undocumented Zimbabwean migrants in 2009-2010, South African immigration policy still lacks provisions to accommodate the legal immigration of African migrants. At the national level, in light of anti-immigrant sentiment among government officials and the public, major reforms will undoubtedly be hard to achieve. Nevertheless, advocates for reform see a potential for change, in part because there is an economic imperative to expand opportunities for legal immigration. Migrants, particularly skilled migrants, are in economic demand, and legal employment has the potential to reduce stigma. There is also scope for public education to combat misinformation, given that most South Africans who hold negative opinions actually have had little or no contact with migrants.

It is likely, however, that incremental measures in this regard, such as the effort to register Zimbabwean migrants in 2010, will continue to be accompanied, as in Europe and the United States, with stepped-up deportations and largely ineffective efforts to tighten border control.

Given structural economic realities and the embedded character of public opinion on the issue, it is virtually certain that these measures will not significantly reduce the growth of the migrant population in South Africa, curtail ongoing human rights violations, nor eliminate the threat of new large-scale violence.

Central and East Africa

Unlike the other three African regions, where dominant migration patterns defined by economic relationships are clearly visible, that is not the case for Central and Eastern Africa. For this reason, as Bakewell and de Haas (2007) note in their survey, most research on migration in these regions has focused on forced migration produced by conflict. Data are particularly scarce on other forms of migration, even though the majority of population movements across borders within the region are not refugees. Flows of migrants, mostly non-refugees, from East and Central Africa to destinations outside Africa are also significant, especially to Europe, the Middle East, and North America.

Neither in Central nor in East Africa, however, do these migration flows seem to form coherent migration systems at the regional level. Transportation networks linking the countries of the region are particularly weak in Central Africa, while in East Africa only the former British territories of Kenya, Tanzania, and Uganda make up a significant multi-country transportation system. Migration outside the continent follows separate colonial, linguistic, and regional trajectories for different countries and sub-regions.

Instead, it is the high proportion of refugees that most strikingly defines the distinct character of these regions, and justifies discussing them together here. Refugees numbered some 930,000 and 1.3 million in the two regions respectively in 2009, according to the United Nations High Commission for Refugees (UNHCR 2010). Refugees were nowhere near the majority of emigrants from these regions: in 2000, there were some 2.7 million emigrants from Central African countries and some 3.3 million emigrants from East African countries (see Table 2; comparable totals on emigrants are not available for later years). But the size of the refugee population, the media attention to refugee-producing crises in these regions, and the involvement of international agencies and non-governmental organizations with refugees has made them particularly visible. For worldwide media audiences, the refugees of Central or East Africa have become emblematic of African migrants not only for these regions but arguably for the continent as a whole.

Four Central and East African countries are among the top ten source countries of refugees worldwide. Somalia ranks third, behind Afghanistan and Iraq, while the Democratic Republic of the Congo ranks fourth. Sudan ranks seventh, and Eritrea ranks ninth.

East and Central Africa also have the largest numbers of internally displaced people in Africa, with an estimated 2.5 million in Central Africa and 3.4 million in East Africa as of 2009 (see Table 6). Internally displaced people have attracted additional attention from international agencies in recent years, and, following a 2005 agreement with other agencies, the UNHCR has formal responsibility for coordinating the international response. Notably, internally displaced people outnumber refugees both at a regional level and in the principal refugee-producing countries (Sudan, the Democratic Republic of the Congo, and Somalia). Those three countries were first, fourth, and fifth respectively among the six largest internally displaced populations worldwide, with 4.9 million, 1.9 million, and 1.5 million respectively (http://www.internal-displacement.org).

The large number of refugees from Central and East African countries is a product of a series of interlocking conflicts in countries of the area, many of which have continued for decades. In terms of scale, the largest have been the conflicts in the Great Lakes region, culminating in the genocide in Rwanda in 1994 and the series of wars in Eastern Congo, the continuing internal conflict in Somalia, and the wars in southern Sudan and Darfur. In Central Africa, conflicts in the Central African Republic and Chad have produced both refugee flows and internal displacement. Although the open war between Eritrea and Ethiopia lasted only two years, ending in 2000, the continuation of hostilities and internal political conflicts in both countries means that the number of refugees and asylum seekers continues to be substantial. There are still some 400,000 internally displaced in Kenya from the aftermath of the 2007 disputed election. In Uganda, more than 400,000 people remain internally displaced after conflict in the north with the Lord's Resistance Army (LRA), although the number has diminished in recent years. The LRA, however, has taken its campaign of violence to neighbouring countries, including the Democratic Republic of the Congo, Central African Republic, and southern Sudan.

Since most refugees go to neighbouring states, East and Central African countries are also among the continent's and the world's largest hosts of refugee populations. The two regions together host some 1.8 million refugees out of the 2.2 million refugees on the continent. Kenya and Chad rank fifth and sixth, respectively, among refugee-hosting countries worldwide.

Despite the existence of international agreements on the rights of refugees and a United Nations agency dedicated to their welfare, widespread violation of these rights attracts little public attention. Whereas housing of refugees in camps was originally conceived as a temporary measure, long-term unresolved crises have led to "warehousing" of refugees for decades at a time, and even for generations (see box). While in recent years, the UN High Commissioner for Refugees has given greater attention to these broader issues (UNHCR 2008),

TABLE 6. REFUGEES, ASYLUM-SEEKERS, INTERNALLY DISPLACED PERSONS (IDPS), AND OTHERS OF CONCERN TO UNHCR BY ORIGIN, END-2009

Origin	Refugees and Asylum Seekers — Total Refugees and People in Refugee-Like Situations	Asylum-Seekers (Pending Cases)	IDPs: Protected/Assisted by UNHCR, incl. People in IDP-Like Situations	Total Population of Concern
North Africa				
Algeria	8,185	1,546	-	9,732
Egypt	6,990	1,638	-	8,629
Libyan Arab Jamahiriya	2,202	641	-	2,843
Morocco	2,286	610	-	2,896
Tunisia	2,260	505	-	2,765
Western Sahara	116,474	21	-	116,495
Total North Africa	**138,397**	**4,961**	**-**	**143,360**
West Africa				
Benin	411	197	-	608
Burkina Faso	990	377	-	1,367
Cape Verde	24	7	-	31
Côte d'Ivoire	23,153	5,277	519,140	714,476
Gambia	1,973	1,165	-	5,294
Ghana	14,893	1,347	-	16,241
Guinea	10,920	2,828	-	13,749
Guinea-Bissau	1,109	338	-	1,447
Liberia	71,599	2,203	-	77,710
Mali	2,926	766	-	3,692
Mauritania	39,143	911	-	52,067
Niger	822	280	-	1,102
Nigeria	15,609	9,663	-	25,272
Senegal	16,305	633	-	16,938
Sierra Leone	15,417	2,949	-	18,593
Togo	18,378	970	-	19,632
Total West Africa	**233,674**	**29,911**	**519,140**	**968,221**
Central Africa				
Burundi	94,239	4,864	100,000	231,465
Cameroon	14,766	2,258	-	17,024
Central African Rep.	159,554	870	197,000	357,477
Chad	55,014	2,321	170,531	250,439
Congo, Rep. of	20,544	3,202	-	23,826
Dem. Rep. of the Congo	455,852	31,126	2,052,677	2,662,821
Equatorial Guinea	344	40	-	384
Gabon	144	48	-	192
Rwanda	129,109	4,812	-	154,517
Sao Tome and Principe	33	-	-	33
Total Central Africa	**929,598**	**49,541**	**2,520,208**	**3,698,177**
East Africa				
Comoros	268	13	-	281
Djibouti	622	162	-	784
Eritrea	209,168	14,394	-	223,570
Ethiopia	62,889	48,739	-	111,645
Kenya	9,620	2,979	399,000	417,052
Madagascar	274	32	-	306
Mauritius	23	17	-	40
Seychelles	49	9	-	58
Somalia	678,309	21,084	1,550,000	2,249,454

Origin	Total Refugees and People in Refugee-Like Situations	Asylum-Seekers (Pending Cases)	IDPs: Protected/Assisted by UNHCR, incl. People in IDP-Like Situations	Total Population of Concern
Sudan	368,195	16,922	1,034,140	1,619,296
Uganda	7,554	909	446,300	862,551
United Rep. of Tanzania	1,204	203	-	156,458
Total East Africa	**1,338,176**	**105,463**	**3,429,440**	**5,641,496**
Southern Africa				
Angola	141,021	699	-	158,648
Botswana	30	197	-	227
Lesotho	10	4	-	14
Malawi	130	46	-	176
Mozambique	136	9	-	145
Namibia	921	48	-	1,000
South Africa	384	170	-	554
Swaziland	32	56	-	88
Zambia	206	54	-	260
Zimbabwe	22,449	1,404	-	23,872
Total Southern Africa	**142,870**	**144,153**	**1,283**	**161,112**
UNHCR-Bureaux				
Central Africa-Great Lakes	930,802	49,744	2,520,208	3,854,635
East and Horn of Africa	1,336,357	105,189	3,429,440	5,484,352
Southern Africa	165,935	2,758	-	185,671
Western Africa	194,530	29,000	519,140	916,153
Asia and Pacific	4,276,792	117,990	2,693,876	8,418,276
Middle East and North Africa	2,099,697	40,719	1,802,003	4,160,211
Europe	724,602	60,146	1,359,411	2,331,662
Americas	465,275	132,954	3,303,979	3,902,278
Various/Stateless	202,550	444,920	-	7,207,068
Total	**10,396,540**	**983,420**	**15,628,057**	**36,460,306**
Region				
Africa	2,805,165	192,563	6,468,788	10,636,239
Asia	6,393,200	173,028	5,434,532	13,624,502
Europe	528,245	39,541	420,758	1,087,700
Latin America and the Caribbean	462,808	131,487	3,303,979	3,898,344
Northern America	2,467	1,467	-	3,934
Oceania	2,105	414	-	2,519
Various/Stateless	202,550	444,920	-	7,207,068
Total	**10,396,540**	**983,420**	**15,628,057**	**36,460,306**

public and private agencies, as well as public opinion, continue to focus on responding to immediate crises to the neglect of such fundamental issues.

The case of Somalia, where internal conflict for almost two decades has provided an uninterrupted stream of refugees, primarily to neighbouring countries, well illustrates the issue. Kenya bears the disproportionate share of the burden, with over 300,000 of the more than 600,000 Somali refugees registered worldwide, along with substantial but unknown numbers of unregistered Somali nationals. According to reports by Human Rights Watch (2009) and Amnesty

Statement Calling for Solutions to End the Warehousing of Refugees

U.S. Committee for Refugees and Immigrants
http://www.refugees.org

September 2009

The 1951 Convention and the 1967 Protocol relating to the Status of Refugees provide that persons fleeing persecution across borders deserve international protection, including freedom from forcible return (*refoulement*) and basic rights necessary for refugees to live a free, dignified, and self-reliant life even while they remain refugees. These rights include the rights to earn a livelihood—to engage in wage-employment, self-employment, the practice of professions, and the ownership of property—freedom of movement and residence, and the issuance of travel documents. These rights are applicable to refugees independently of whether a durable solution, such as voluntary repatriation, third-country resettlement, or naturalization in the country of first asylum, is available. They are part of the protection mandate of the United Nations High Commissioner for Refugees (UNHCR).

Of the nearly 14 million refugees in the world today, nearly 9 million are warehoused, confined to camps or segregated settlements or otherwise deprived of these basic rights, in situations lasting 10 years or more. Warehousing refugees not only violates their rights but also often reduces refugees to enforced idleness, dependency, and despair.

In light of the foregoing, the undersigned:

1. denounce the practice of warehousing refugees as a denial of rights in violation of the letter and spirit of the 1951 Convention and 1967 Protocol and call upon the international community, including donor countries, host countries and members of the Executive Committee of UNHCR to do the same;
2. call upon the international community to develop and implement strategies to end the practice of warehousing, including examining how refugee assistance can enable the greater enjoyment of Convention rights;
3. call upon UNHCR to monitor refugee situations more effectively for the realization of all the rights of refugees under the Convention, including those related to freedom of movement and the right to earn a livelihood;
4. call upon those countries that have not yet ratified the Convention or the Protocol to do so;
5. call upon those countries that have ratified the Convention and/or the Protocol but have done so with reservations on key articles pertaining to the right to work and freedom of movement to remove those reservations; and
6. call upon all countries to pass legislation, promulgate policies, and implement programs providing for the full enjoyment of the basic rights of refugees as set forth in the Convention.

International (2010), both the international community and the Kenyan government have failed to protect the rights of these refugees. As of early 2010, camps in Kenya originally built for 90,000 refugees house more than 250,000, and residents are confined to the camps by a de facto prohibition on freedom of movement. By closing the border, returning refugees, and otherwise restricting the rights of refugees, the Kenyan government has aggravated humanitarian conditions in the camps and violated the rights of Somali refugees and asylum-seekers elsewhere in the country.[16]

Given that resolution of the crisis in Somalia does not appear imminent, the situation of Somali refugees must be addressed. Conditions in Kenya need to be improved. At the same time, the international community should take up a greater share of the burden of supporting and receiving Somali refugees, with provisions for increased resettlement beyond Kenya. The situation serves as a stark reminder of the long-term structural failure to implement existing international commitments for protection of refugee rights.

---

16. See also the reports on Somali refugees from Refugees International (http://www.refugeesinternational.org/where-we-work/africa/somalia).

MIGRATION FRAMEWORKS: INTERNATIONAL AND INTERNAL

Although it is now less prominent in migration scholarship, the classic "push-pull" concept of the causes of migration continues to dominate popular discussion of international migration. This view separates the factors promoting migration into two sets: the negative "push" factors impelling migrants to leave their countries of origin, and the positive "pull" factors attracting them to destination countries. Although the distinction has a common-sense plausibility, it has at least two significant limitations. As a metaphor it promotes a physics-based image of migrants as passive objects moved by opposing forces rather than as active decision-making agents. Second, it compartmentalizes the analysis of origin and destination countries, seeing them as separate and opposed rather than looking at the social, political, and economic relationships between them as key to the development of migratory networks.

With international migration a growing issue on all continents, and current scholars stressing the impact of globalisation, it is time to explore alternative frameworks that go beyond push-pull. In the process, we need to examine other traditional dichotomies in the study of migration. Distinctions such as "voluntary" and "forced" migration, "political" and "economic" migration, "legal" and "illegal" migration, and even "internal" and "international" migration do call attention to diversities in migration. But they may also obscure commonalities in the forces at work, and they create artificially distinct categories where the reality is fuzzy at best.[17]

This essay does not attempt to present a full-fledged alternative framework, a task best pursued by scholars specializing in migration studies.[18] However, it is possible to call attention to several general assumptions and more specific themes that should be integrated into any such framework.

In contrast to seeing migration as something exceptional or abnormal, it should be seen as a normal part of human existence, as something people consider among various options for improving their current situation and future opportunities. Decisions about whether to move, how far, when, under what circumstances, and at what costs depend on a multitude of factors, from individual preferences to local, national, and international contexts. But people who migrate (and those who don't) consider the options they are aware of, weigh them against each other, and make their choices. Any viable framework for understanding migration must take into account not only external contexts but also human choice.

---

17. For a summary description of theoretical frameworks on migration, with additional references, see Castles and Miller (2009: 20-49).
18. The publication of the 2009 Human Development Report (UNDP 2009) and associated research papers is a landmark in this process.

This section considers the growing recognition of commonalities between internal and international migration. Subsequent sections consider several other themes, namely the relationships between migration and global inequalities, migration and development, and migration and human rights.

While the international legal framework for refugees has been well defined for over half a century, it is only in the last two decades that international attention has extended the focus to the new related category of "internally displaced persons" (IDPs). Primary responsibility for care of such persons displaced within borders remains with their state of residence, and their situation is not clearly delineated in international law. But both institutional and conceptual assumptions have changed significantly. The UNHCR has assumed responsibility for IDPs in many although not all cases, particularly those due to internal violence. Although they are not legally binding, a set of Guiding Principles on Internal Displacement was adopted by UN agencies in 1998. And the African Union, in October 2009, adopted the African Union Convention for the Protection and Assistance of Internally Displaced Persons in Africa (the "Kampala Convention"), which is still in the early stages of ratification by member countries.[19]

These standards, which are still evolving, are part of a trend toward acceptance of greater international responsibility for human rights violations within countries under the rubric of "responsibility to protect" (R2P)[20]. They also mark wide recognition that the situation of IDPs and that of refugees pose many of the same issues, whether in terms of the causes of displacement or the measures needed to cope with its effects.

Nevertheless, both practice and debate still feature many gaps. The debate on R2P has been overwhelmingly dominated by the option of international military intervention, on which it is particularly difficult to reach consensus, as well as by the practical issues of delivering humanitarian assistance. Largely neglected, and in need of systematic attention, are the issues of preventive action and of sustainable solutions following displacement (Cohen 2010; Barbour and Gorlick 2008). This major fault, it is worth noting, applies both to IDPs and to refugees. Similarly, the issue of sustainable funding for both refugees and internally displaced persons has not been addressed. Financing depends on voluntary financing from governments and from nongovernmental organizations, which varies strongly in proportion to the international media attention attracted by a particular crisis.

---

19. For these and other related documents, see http://www.unhcr.org/refworld/idps.html.
20. This concept, introduced by the International Commission on Intervention and State Sovereignty (ICISS) in 2001, has greatly expanded the acceptance of shared international responsibility to respond to gross human rights abuses, despite state sovereignty. The concept was adopted by the United Nations General Assembly in 2005. See http://www.responsibility-toprotect.org for additional background and documentation.

Additional limitations on international agendas come from the fact that the refugee regime and international responsibility for internal displacement are generally taken as limited to cases of political violence. Even natural disasters are not generally considered in this context, although voluntary international contributions for highly publicized disasters are common. While the 1998 UN Guiding Principles on Internal Displacement include natural disasters, the UN General Assembly's adoption of the Responsibility to Protect in 2005 excluded those displaced by such disasters. And despite the growing international discussion of the impact of climate change and the concept of "climate refugees" (see, in particular, Gemenne, 2011, and additional sources cited there), this discourse has not yet been integrated into the consideration of responsibility for refugees and internally displaced people.

This reflects a general unwillingness to expand the borders of "forced migration," as well as the persistence of the dichotomy between "forced migration" and "economic migration." Faced with limitations on legal immigration opportunities, international migrants increasingly seek entry under the rubric of "asylum-seekers." In response, countries of destination are keen to distinguish between "genuine" refugees and "economic migrants," and highly reluctant to expand the possible grounds for seeking asylum as refugees.

Yet while such distinctions continue to be made on bureaucratic and legal grounds, in conceptual terms the definition of "forced" migration, and consequently the responsibility to protect, cannot possibly be limited to displacement due to violence or even to displacement due to violence and natural disasters. The forces giving rise to migration, it is becoming more and more apparent, are global as well as local. Farmers may be driven off their land by competition from subsidized crops imported from industrialized countries. Or their harvests may fail because of floods or drought, possibly linked to climate change. In either case, they may move to cities and become low-wage labourers, informal peddlers, or unemployed slum residents. It is not at all clear at what point a subsequent decision to cross a border in search of better alternatives stops being voluntary and becomes "forced." And even in cases which are clearly voluntary, surely it is time to begin to question the denial of people's right to move in a world in which movements of goods, money, and ideas face fewer and fewer impediments.

The desire to migrate, indeed, is so pervasive that calling it all "forced" would not be meaningful. Gallup surveys in more than 100 countries since 2008, for example, show that some 700 million people say they would "like to move permanently to another country."[21] Those saying they would want to do so include both rich and poor in countries at all levels of development, and dis-

---

21. Periodic reports on these polls are available on http://www.gallup.com. The one with the 700 million figure is dated Febuary 18, 2010 and entitled "What Makes 700 Million Adults Want to Migrate."

proportionately the young and better educated in each country. Of respondents who have household family members in another country, fully a third say they would want to move.

Gallup reports only provide limited data on the reasons given for potential migrants, and of course only a fraction of those saying they would like to move actually report plans to do so. But Gallup's "potential net migration index," comparing the likely population changes should everyone who wants to move do so, gives an idea of the disparities between countries of destination and countries of origin. Developed countries have positive net migration indexes, such as 160% for Canada, 60% for the United States, and 39% for Western and Southern EU countries (Esipova et al. 2010). Developing regions have negative net migration indexes, with African regions ranging from -8% (Southern Africa) to -38% (West Africa).[22] Within Southern Africa, Botswana (39%) and South Africa (13%) have positive net migration indexes, and Namibia and Zambia marginally positive indexes. But countries like Zimbabwe (-47%), Malawi (-42%), and Mozambique (-26%) have strongly negative indexes.

Even with more finely grained data on the reasons for wishing to migrate, or for actually doing so, which might be forthcoming from Gallup in the future, it would be difficult to draw a precise line between migration decisions that are "forced" or "voluntary." But countries with very high negative indexes certainly indicate conditions that make economic survival and opportunities in the countries themselves extraordinarily difficult. And this means that many of those who do decide to migrate have indeed faced choices that can be fairly described as forced.

---

22. The index is -17% for North Africa, –33% for East Africa, and -36% for Central Africa.

MIGRATION AND GLOBAL INEQUALITIES

For states, the distinction between internal and international migration is fundamental. For migrants themselves, however, it is only one of many factors to take into account when deciding whether to move or stay, and where to move if the decision is made to move.

The basic dynamics of international migration involve the same elements as internal migration: the different opportunities that are available and known to potential migrants, whether the migration channel is one that is familiar and well trodden, what networks of contacts are available to assist, the costs and risks, and the anticipated gains. Whether migration is internal or international, individuals, household, or extended families do not make one single choice, but often employ mixed strategies, including migration at different stages of life and by different members of a household or family.

Despite the diversity of factors involved and the geographic dispersion of migration streams, structural inequalities play a large role in shaping the scale and the direction of migration everywhere. Internally displaced people and asylum seekers move toward zones of greater physical security. More generally, migrants move away from regions with fewer opportunities toward regions with more. Urbanization proceeds apace on all continents. Within countries, zones where economic activity is waning lose population. Across borders, the increase in migration, although it still accounts for only 3 percent of world population, is linked to forces that are unlikely to be reversed.

Economist Lant Pritchett (2006: 5–7) summarizes this convergence in what he terms "five irresistible forces":

- Gaps in unskilled wages, often of ratios as high as 10 to 1, between receiving and sending countries. This compares with gaps between 2 to 1 and 4 to 1 in the 19th century, which were themselves sufficient to induce massive migration flows.
- Differing demographic futures, with declining working-age populations in receiving regions such as Europe.
- Globalization of everything except labour, as flows of goods, capital, ideas, and communication increase far faster than flows of people.
- Rise in employment in low-skill "non-tradable" service jobs, which cannot be outsourced (think, for example, of trash collection), with consequent demand for unskilled labour even in the most advanced "world cities."
- Lagging growth in countries particularly disadvantaged by environmental and economic shocks.

Scholars dispute whether or not global inequality has increased in recent decades.[23] However, there is no dispute that the levels of global inequality are extremely high, whether measured by income, wealth, or more comprehensive indexes such as the Human Development Index. Several scholars, particularly Branko Milanovic, Roberto Korzeniewicz, and Timothy Moran, have explored the changes in global inequality over a longer period, and noted the implications for migration. Like class, one's location is determined at birth. Together, notes Milanovic (2009b: 24), class and location explain some 80 percent of income variability; other less quantifiable factors determined at birth, such as gender, race, and ethnicity, likely account for additional differences. Personal effort and luck, therefore, are likely to account for less than one-fifth of the differences in people's incomes.

Comparing the relative contribution of class and location, Milanovic estimates that in the early 19th century, roughly 35 percent of differences in income was due to differences between countries, while some 65 percent was due to within-country differences. In the early 21st century, the proportions were more than reversed, with 85 to 90 percent due to differences between countries and 10 to 15 percent due to within-country differences. Over the same period, the overall level of global inequality grew from a Gini index of 43 (slightly more equal than the 45 Gini index for the United States) to a Gini index of 70, This is a higher level of inequality than the 65 Gini index for South Africa, which is among the highest in the world.

Scholars will continue to debate the precise numbers in such estimates, which are at best rough approximations. However, the importance of place of birth as a determinant of one's life chances is an unavoidable conclusion once one begins to consider global stratification rather than only stratification within countries. The difference in wages and other opportunities between countries holds not only for unskilled labour but at almost all levels of the occupational and social ladder, with the exception of the "super-rich" (many of whom have residences and other assets spread among multiple countries). The result, note Korzeniewicz and Moran (2009: 101) is that:

> From a global perspective, there are three main paths to social mobility: (1) a change (up or down) in the relative position of individuals or groups within national income distributions; (2) a change in the relative position of nations within the international income distribution; or (3) a shift in the relative location of individuals or groups within the global distribution of income attained through categorical mobility [i.e. moving from one country to another].

---

23. See Milanovic (2005) for a review of the issues, which include measurement questions, as well as the specific role of large countries such as India and China.

But the third option should be considered not as movement from one closed box to another, but as part of a continuum. Table 7, adapted from Korzeniewicz and Moran, is helpful in envisaging a more nuanced set of alternatives, arranging income deciles from 85 countries on one global scale.[24] Looking at the table, one can see how industrialized countries are concentrated in the upper deciles and African countries in particular concentrated in the lower deciles. The highest (10th) decile for Nigeria, Kenya, and Burkina Faso, for example, is located in the 7th global decile. It is below the lowest (1st) decile in the United States, Italy, Australia, and many other industrialized countries, which are located globally in the 9th global decile.

A simplistic "push-pull" model might lead one to think that the poorest people would be the most likely to migrate from one country to another. But in fact migration, whether internal and international, requires resources; witness those left behind in New Orleans during the Hurricane Katrina disaster. The sharp inequality between countries makes moving internationally an attractive alternative particularly for those who are already mobile geographically and economically within their countries. Their contacts and other resources make such a choice feasible.

For African migrants, as for migrants in most cases around the world, those who migrate are predominantly not the poorest but those who are well enough off to afford the costs of moving, but who find themselves unemployed, underemployed, or lacking opportunities to improve their living conditions. And most take the initiative themselves, rather than being recruited by smugglers. While they may make use of agents to pass particularly difficult borders, migrants themselves are the ones who put the pieces together for complex and often multi-stage migration journeys. International migration, just as internal migration from countryside to city or from poorer areas to richer ones, is one of the repertoire of options that people use to improve their opportunities and the opportunities of their families.

The parallel between the forces at work in internal and international migration can also be seen by analysing systems in which states have attempted to control internal migration by imposing internal borders and restrictions of movement. The most notorious example, of course, is the South African apartheid system. That system is often envisaged merely as a system of racial separation. But it was also an elaborately constructed system of labour control, as "pass laws" defined the rights of Africans to live and work in specific areas. Workers on temporary contracts but without rights were channelled to places where labour was needed, to be used and then returned to "homelands" and neighbour-

---

24. For comparison, average income has been added in brackets for a number of countries for which decile data is not available.

African Migration, Global Inequalities, and Human Rights

TABLE 7. GLOBAL STRATIFICATION: 850 COUNTRY DECILES RANKED FROM RICH TO POOR

Global Deciles and Estimated per capita GNI, 2007

Adapted from Figure 5.1 in Korzeniewicz and Moran, 2008: 92.

Note: Developed countries in the table are marked in bold. African countries in the table are marked in bold italic.

$164,700

10th (top) Global Decile

Norway-10 Luxembourg-10 Switzerland-10 USA-10 Ireland-10 UK-10 Luxembourg-9 Denmark-10 Norway-9 Sweden-10 Canada-10 Belgium-10 Finland-10 Luxembourg-8 Austria-10 Norway-8 Netherlands-10 Switzerland-9 Germany-10 France-10 Italy-10 Australia-10 Luxembourg-7 Norway-7 Denmark-9 Spain-10 Norway-6 Switzerland-8 Greece-10 Luxembourg-6 Ireland-9 USA-9 Norway-5 UK-9 Denmark-8 Sweden-9 Netherlands-9 Luxembourg-5 Switzerland-7 Ireland-8 Finland-9 Norway-4 Denmark-7 Austria-9 Canada-9 Belgium-9 USA-8 Luxembourg-4 France-9 Switzerland-6 Israel-10 Germany-9 Netherlands-8 Sweden-8 Australia-9 Denmark-6 UK-8 Norway-3 Finland-8 Ireland-7 Austria-8 Portugal-10 Italy-9 Denmark-5 Switzerland-5 Luxembourg-3 Netherlands-7 Canada-8 Sweden-7 Belgium-8 USA-7 Finland-7 Germany-8 France-8 Ireland-6 Australia-8 Austria-7 Greece-9 Korea-10 Spain-9 UK-7 Netherlands-6 Norway-2 Denmark-4 Switzerland-4 Sweden-6 Finland-6 Belgium-7 Canada-7 Luxembourg-2 Slovenia-10 Taiwan-10 Italy-8 USA-6 Austria-6 Germany-7 Netherlands-5 France-7 Sweden-5 Ireland-5 Australia-7 Belgium-6 Switzerland-3 Finland-5 Denmark-3 UK-6 Greece-8 Chile-10 Austria-5 Spain-8 Canada-6 Germany-6 Netherlands-4 Estonia-10 Sweden-4 Italy-7 France-6 USA-5 Israel-9 Belgium-5 Finland-4 Ireland-4 Australia-6 Mexico-10 Germany-5 Austria-4 UK-5 Denmark-2 Switzerland-2 Greece-7 Canada-5 Netherlands-3 France-5 Sweden-3 Czech Republic-10 Spain-7 Luxembourg-1 Croatia-10 Italy-6 Belgium-4 Korea-9 Finland-3 Norway-1 Slovenia-9 USA-4 Germany-4 Australia-5 Latvia-10 Austria-3 Portugal-9 France-4

[Other countries with national average GNI per capita in this range, for which comparable decile data was unavailable, include Japan, at $34,620.]

$27,894 Israel-8

9th Global Decile

Netherlands-2 Canada-4 Hungary-10 Greece-6 UK-4 Ireland-3 Brazil-10 Spain-6 Taiwan-9 Sweden-2 Italy-5 Lithuania-10 Finland-2 Belgium-3 Malaysia-10 Germany-3 Slovenia-8 Korea-8 France-3 Australia-4 Austria-2 Russia-10 Denmark-1 Israel-7 USA-3 Slovakia-10 Greece-5 Canada-3 Poland-10 Spain-5 Slovenia-7 Venezuela-10 Portugal-8 Panama-10 UK-3 Italy-4 Taiwan-8 Argentina-10 Belgium-2 Korea-7 Germany-2 Ireland-2 Estonia-9 Switzerland-1 France-2 Slovenia-6 Czech Republic-9 Uruguay-10 Australia-3 Greece-4 Israel-6 Spain-4 Netherlands-1 Portugal-7 Taiwan-7 Finland-1 Italy-3 Canada-2 Slovenia-5 Korea-6 Costa Rica-10 UK-2 Suriname-10 USA-2 Sweden-1 Czech Republic-8 Portugal-6 Hungary-9 Israel-5 Korea-5 Taiwan-6 Slovenia-4 Australia-2 Greece-3 Spain-3 Estonia-8 Slovakia-9 Jamaica-10 Croatia-9 Austria-1 Italy-2 Portugal-5 Czech Republic-7 Lithuania-9 Latvia-9 Belgium-1 Thailand-10 Belize-10 Poland-9 Korea-4 Taiwan-5 Ireland-1 Slovenia-3 Colombia-10 France-1 Slovakia-8 Romania-10 Israel-4 Dominican Republic-10 Ecuador-10 Hungary-8 Peru-10 Estonia-7 Czech Republic-6 Germany-1 Portugal-4 Mexico-9 Greece-2 Spain-2 Taiwan-4 Russia-9 Slovakia-7 Chile-9 Croatia-8 Poland-8 Lithuania-8 Korea-3 Czech Republic-5 Hungary-7 Venezuela-9 Slovenia-2 UK-1 Slovakia-6 Latvia-8 Israel-3 Estonia-6 Taiwan-3 Bulgaria-10 Canada-1 Czech Republic-4 Poland-7 El Salvador-10 Malaysia-9 Croatia-7 Australia-1 Hungary-6 Uruguay-9 Slovakia-5 Lithuania-7 Argentina-9 Guatemala-10 USA-1 Estonia-5 Czech Republic-3 Brazil-9 Portugal-3 Latvia-7 Slovakia-4 Poland-6 Hungary-5 Russia-8 Panama-9 Mexico-8 Taiwan-2 Venezuela-8 Costa Rica-9 Israel-2 Lithuania-6 Croatia-6 Belarus-10 Romania-9 Italy-1 Korea-2 Chile-8 Czech Republic-2 Slovakia-3 Estonia-4 Sri Lanka-10 Poland-5 Suriname-9 Latvia-6 Hungary-4

[Other countries with national average GNI per capita in this range, for which comparable decile data was unavailable, include Saudi Arabia, at $8,150.]

$7,898 Spain-1

45

8th Global Decile

Lithuania-5 Uruguay-8 Russia-7 Croatia-5 Portugal-2 Slovenia-1 China-10 Malaysia-8 Greece-1 Romania-8 Venezuela-7 Argentina-8 Mexico-7 Latvia-5 Poland-4 Hungary-3 Paraguay-10 *Egypt-10* Slovakia-2 Estonia-3 Costa Rica-8 Bulgaria-9 Lithuania-4 Honduras-10 Latvia-4 Croatia-4 Philippines-10 Romania-9 Panama-8 Chile-7 Jamaica-9 Hungary-2 Uruguay-7 Brazil-8 Russia-6 Thailand-9 Taiwan-1 Venezuela-6 Czech Republic-1 Poland-3 Israel-1 Bolivia-10 Mexico-6 Belarus-9 Belize-9 Romania-6 Latvia-3 Dominican Republic-9 Malaysia-7 Portugal-1 Lithuania-3 Estonia-2 Argentina-7 Bulgaria-8 *Lesotho-10* Peru-9 Suriname-8 Costa Rica-7 Croatia-3 Indonesia-10 Romania-5 Chile-6 Uruguay-6 *Cameroon-10* Colombia-9 *Mauritania-10* Venezuela-5 Russia-S Belarus-8 Panama-7 Bulgaria-7 El Salvador-9 Mexico-5 Poland-2 Romania-4 Brazil-7 *Zambia-10* Malaysia-6 Ecuador-9 Latvia-2 Argentina-6 Costa Rica-6 Belarus-7 Jamaica-8 Lithuania-2 Slovakia-1 Hungary-1 Nicaragua-10 Uruguay-5 Belize-8 China-9 Bulgaria-6 Chile-5

$4,179 Korea-1

7th Global Decile

Venezuela-4 Russia-4 Croatia-2 Dominican Republic-8 Suriname-7 Belarus-6 Romania-3 Thailand-8 Peru-S *Nigeria-10* Moldova-10 Panama-6 Mexico-4 Bulgaria-5 India-10 Guatemala-9 Costa Rica-5 Malaysia-5 Belarus-5 Argentina-5 Uruguay-4 Brazil-6 Colombia-8 Chile-4 El Salvador-8 Belize-7 Estonia-1 Romania-2 Bulgaria-4 Venezuela-3 Suriname-6 Jamaica-7 Belarus-4 Russia-3 Ecuador-8 China-8 Dominican Republic-7 Peru-7 Costa Rica-4 Mexico-3 Belarus-3 Panama-5 Malaysia-4 *Kenya-10 Burkina Faso-10* Argentina-4 Uruguay-3 Bulgaria-3 Thailand-7 Brazil-5 Suriname-5 Chile-3 Honduras-9 Belize-6 Haiti-10 Paraguay-9 El Salvador-7 Colombia-7 Uzbekistan-10 Guatemala-8 Philippines-9 Belarus-2 Indonesia-9 Jamaica-6 Croatia-1 Latvia-1 Dominican Republic-6 Ecuador-7 Venezuela-2 Peru-6 Costa Rica-3

[Other countries with national average GNI per capita in this range, for which comparable decile data was unavailable, include Mauritius ($3,870), Botswana ($3,180), and South Africa ($3,050).]

$2,377 China-7

6th Global Decile

Russia-2 *Guinea-10 Egypt-9* Malaysia-3 Panama-4 *Ghana-10* Poland-1 Bulgaria-2 Romania-1 Belize-5 Argentina-3 Suriname-4 Brazil-4 Uruguay-2 Chile-2 Mexico-2 El Salvador-6 *Zimbabwe-10* Colombia-6 Thailand-6 Bolivia-9 Moldova-9 Guatemala-7 *Central African Republic-10* Dominican Republic-5 Ecuador-6 *Gambia-10* Lithuanaia-1 Peru-5 Jamaica-5 Indonesia-8 Honduras-8 Belarus-1 Paraguay-8 China-6 Philippines-8 Belize-4 Sri Lanka-9 Costa Rica-2 Malaysia-2 El Salvador-5 *Lesotho-9* Colombia-5 Guatemala-6 Brazil-3 India-9 Ecuador-5 *Cameroon-9* Dominican Republic-4 Panama-3 *Egypt-8* Argentina-2 Suriname-3 Moldova-8 Peru-4 *Madagascar-10*

[Other countries with national average GNI per capita in this range, for which comparable decile data was unavailable, include Algeria, at $1,810.]

$1,547 Indonesia-7

5th Global Decile

Thailand-5 *Uganda-10* Bangladesh-10 Belize-3 Nicaragua-9 *Nigeria-9* Paraguay-7 Nepal-10 China-5 Honduras-7 Philippines-7 Bolivia-8 Jamaica-4 El Salvador-4 Guatemala-5 Colombia-4 Sri Lanka-8 Bulgaria-1 Indoesia-6 Ecuador-4 Venezuela-1 Uruguay-1 Dominican Republic-3 Moldova-7 *Egypt-7* Uzbekistan-9 Chile-1 *Mauritania-9* Peru-3 Brazil-2 Paraguay-6 Thailand-4 Suriname-2 *Kenya-9* Indonesia-5 China-4

$1,104 India-8

African Migration, Global Inequalities, and Human Rights

4th Global Decile

Cameroon-8 Zambia-9 Russia-1 Guatemala-4 Philippines-6 Sri Lanka-7 Moldova-6 Honduras-6 Bolivia-7 Malaysia-1 Belize-2 Nicaragua-8 Colombia-3 El Salvador-3 Ecuador-3 Mexico-1 *Nigeria-8 Egypt-6 Ghana-9 Lesotho-8* Panama-2 Indonesia-4 Dominican Republic-2 *Ethiopia-10* Uzbekistan-8 Paraguay-5 China-3 Sri Lanka-6 Moldova-5 Philippines-5 Costa Rica-1 Haiti-9 Guatemala-3 Jamaica-3 Peru-2 *Egypt-5* India-7 Indonesia-3 Argentina-1 Thailand-3 Bolivia-6 Honduras-s *Cameroon-7 Kenya-8* Nicaragua-7 *Nigeria-7 Mauritania-8* Bangladesh-9 Ecuador-2 Moldova-4 Sri Lanka-5 *Zambia-8* Uzbekistan-7 Philippines-4 *Ghana-8* Paraguay-4 Colombia-2 *Egypt-4*

$666 China-2

3rd Global Decile

Indonesia-2 El Salvador-2 *Guinea-9* India-6 Guatemala-2 Bolivia-5 Nicaragua-6 *Lesotho-7 Cameroon-6 Central African Republic-9* Honduras-4 *Nigeria-6* Brazil-1 Moldova-3 *Burkina Faso-9* Kenya-7 Sri Lanka-4 Haiti-8 Philippines-3 Uzbekistan-6 Nepal-9 Bangladesh-8 *Madagascar-9 Ghana-7 Egypt-3* Thailand-2 *Mauritania-7* Paraguay-3 *Zambia-7 Uganda-9* Suriname-1 India-5 Nicaragua-5 Dominican Republic-1 *Nigeria-5 Zimbabwe-9 Cameroon-5 Gambia-9* Moldova-2 Uzbekistan-5 *Kenya-6* Honduras-3 Indonesia-1

$443 Bangladesh-7

2nd Global Decile

Bolivia-4 Philippines-2 Sri Lanka-3 Belize-1 Peru-1 Haiti-7 *Ghana-6 Lesotho-6* China-1 Nicaragua-4 India-4 Nepal-8 *Nigeria-4* Jamaica-2 *Central African Republic-8 Egypt-2 Zambia-6* Bangladesh-6 Panama-1 *Cameroon-4 Madagascar-4* Ecuador-1 Uzbekistan-4 *Mauritania-6 Guinea-8 Uganda-8 Kenya-5 Ghana-5* Haiti-6 India-3 Paraguay-2 Nicaragua-3 Bangladesh-5 *Nigeria-3 Ethiopia-9 Burkina Faso-8* Nepal-7 Guatemala-1 Honduras-2 Philippines-1 *Zambia-5* Sri Lanka-2 Bolivia-3 *Lesotho-5 Zimbabwe-8* Bangladesh-4

$266 Uzbekistan-3

1st (bottom) Global Decile

Colombia-l *Ghana-4* Haiti-5 *Uganda-7 Central African Republic-7 Cameroon-3 Kenya-4 Gambia-8 Madagascar-7* Moldova-1 India-2 *Nigeria-2* Nepal-6 *Mauritania-5* Nicaragua-2 El Salvador-1 *Ethiopia-8* Bangladesh-3 *Zambia-4 Uganda-6* Haiti-4 *Guinea-7 Ghana-3 Lesotho-4 Zimbabwe-7 Egypt-1* Kenya-3 *Central African Republic-6* Nepal-5 *Burkina Faso-7* Thailand-1 Uzbekistan-2 *Madagascar-6 Ethiopia-7* Bangladesh-2 *Uganda-5 Gambia-7 Cameroon-2* Haiti-3 *Mauritania-4 Zambia-3 Ethiopia-6* Honduras-1 Nepal-4 *Uganda-4 Guinea-6 Ghana-2 Nigeria-1 Zimbabwe-6 Lesotho-3 Central African Republic-5* Paraguay-1 *Madagascar-5* India-1 *Ethiopia-5 Burkina Faso-6 Gambia-6* Nicaragua-1 *Kenya-2* Bolivia-2 *Uganda-3* Haiti-2 *Guinea-5 Ethiopia-4 Central African Republic-4 Mauritania-3* Nepal-3 Bangladesh-1 Zambia-2 Jamaica-1 *Madagascar-4 Zimbabwe-5* Sri Lanka-1 *Burkina Faso-5 Lesotho-2 Gambia-5 Ethiopia-3 Uganda-2* Uzbekistan-1 Guinea-4 Cameroon-1 Central African Republic-3 Ethiopia-2 Burkina Faso-4 Madagascar-3 Zimbabwe-4 Nepal-2 *Ghana-1 Gambia-4 Mauritania-2 Guinea-3 Kenya-1 Central African Republic-2 Uganda-1 Burkina Faso-3 Lesotho-l Gambia-3 Guinea-2* Haiti-1 *Madagascar-2 Zimbabwe-3 Ethiopia-1 Zambia-1* Bolivia-1 *Gambia-2 Burkina Faso-2* Nepal-1 *Central African Republic-1 Mauritania-1 Guinea-1 Zimbabwe-2 Madagascar-1 Gambia-1 Burkina Faso-1 Zimbabwe-1*

$5

ing countries. Workers with special skills were given more permanent rights to reside in urban areas, albeit without political rights. But even the force of the apartheid state at its height and regular removals of "surplus people" were insufficient to stop migration.

The less well known "hukou" system in China, intended to limit rural to urban migration, also illustrates how geographic inequality drives migration even when restrictions on movement are enforced by legal barriers (UNDP 2009: 52; Chan and Buckingham 2008; Amnesty International 2007). Although the system, which allocates rights to employment, housing, and social services, has become more flexible in recent decades, and additional reforms are being discussed, it is still the case that almost all internal migrants lack full rights in urban areas. A significant proportion of migrants lack proper documentation for temporary residence, risking arrest, imprisonment, or deportation to their home areas.

In Africa and around the world, use of coercion to control internal population movement and settlement has proved ineffective, even when it includes such drastic measures as slum clearance and forced evictions. Instead, it has heightened vulnerability of migrants and reinforced inequalities both within and between geographic areas. For international migration, likewise, despite the political appeal of more restrictive measures in many receiving countries, the promise of "control" is likely to be elusive. Such measures may well raise the cost and risk of migration, shift migration from regular to irregular channels, or divert migrants from one destination country to another. They certainly tend to increase the scale of human rights abuses against migrants. What they will not do is to stop the trend of increasing migration in an unequal world, any more than internal controls have stopped rural to urban migration within countries.

The option of reducing migration by promoting development in countries of origin may be more sensitive to human rights concerns and may bring benefits to developing countries. But it is unlikely to succeed on a sufficient scale to reduce migration. It may even increase it, by increasing the proportion of persons in developing countries with sufficient assets to move. This option also fails to question the assumption that migration in itself is a problem. While it may provide an attractive option for receiving and sending countries, it fails to address the rights of migrants and potential migrants.

Seeking "win-win-win" alternatives, as suggested by the 2009 Human Development Report, is by no means an easy quest. But one prerequisite is to shift the focus away from seeing migration itself as the problem. By recognizing migration as an indispensable component of human freedom and human development, one can reduce the chances that migration, whether internal or international, will be accompanied by human rights abuses, conflicts of interest, and reinforcement of hostile stereotypes.

If migration itself is seen as the problem, migrants will inevitably be the victims of policies to reduce migration, as successive control measures fail. "Win-win-win" migration, on the other hand, implies goals that may be difficult but are not inherently impossible. Potential migrants should not be forced to remain in an area, nor be compelled by unbearable circumstances to leave, but should be able to make real choices to go or to stay. Emigration should not drain the sending country of human resources, and immigration should not increase inequality and social conflict within the receiving country. Reducing migration that has such negative effects is no less complicated a goal than reducing migration as such. But it is one which does not deny the reality that migration will continue.

The problem is not migration as such, but inequalities in human development and in access to fundamental human rights, both within and between societies. The following sections explore issues that arise from such an alternative framework. In considering the relationship between migration and development, for example, the issue is not only the development of the societies of origin, but the human development of migrants themselves and equitable relationships between societies of origin and destination. Understanding the nexus between migration and human rights requires addressing not only the rights of migrants but also universal human rights, which apply to all persons regardless of their location, citizenship, or legal status. And the topic of advocacy agendas addresses the extraordinarily difficult question of how to increase the chances that "win-win-win" migration agendas can gain traction within highly unfavourable political and public opinion climates in countries of destination.

MIGRATION AND DEVELOPMENT

Although the development debate continues to focus on macroeconomic growth, as well as on achievement of anti-poverty targets such as the Millennium Development Goals, over two decades the annual UNDP human development reports have encouraged expansion of the range of objectives to consider (http://hdr.undp.org/en/reports/). The 2009 Human Development Report, focusing on migration, laid out an agenda to enhance human development outcomes for movers and for countries of origin and destination. The 2010 Human Development Report, concentrating on inequality within countries, made the case that internal inequality in itself impedes human development.[25]

This brief review of specific issues related to migration and development offers no new policy solutions. The objective is rather to illustrate how a human development framework, combined with consideration of global inequalities, can provide a broader context for policy debate. Developing "win-win-win" policies on migration requires building a consensus in favour of "inequality-reducing" human development. In short, development should be redistributive, both globally and within countries.

The challenge of measuring global inequality, or other inequalities based on units other than countries is, of course, substantial, since statistics are based on national boundaries. Thus one can relatively easily generate measures within a specific country or between countries. But finding comparable measures for groups that overlap country borders, such as people born in a specific country (including those now in the diaspora), is more difficult. Nevertheless, the first step is to call attention to the need to do so. Migration systems and networks, as well as specific processes such as the transfer of remittances, operate both within and across national boundaries. In order to understand the dynamics at work, it is important to consider the wider set of relationships, including inequalities, between sending countries and receiving countries. Thus, whether in binational or multinational terms, one might advance migration within the broader policy goals of reducing inequalities. One might develop a measure of inequality across the countries within a migration system, such as Western Europe-North Africa, or within the Southern African region, combining within-country and between-country inequality as in the measures of global inequality discussed above.

Or, while maintaining the focus on a particular sending country, one could develop measures of "income per natural" as well as "income per resident." As

---

25. Although they confine their study to developed countries, comparing countries as well as states within the United States, Wilkinson and Pickett (2009) in *The Spirit Level* make a strong case that inequality has multiple negative effects not only for those on the bottom ranks but also for human development outcomes for other societal strata and for society as a whole.

advanced by Clemens and Pritchett (2008), such a measure would look at the income for the population born in a specific country, including both residents and migrants living outside the country. Such a measure might indicate, as Clemens and Pritchett argue, that migration is one of the most important means of poverty reduction for a large portion of the developing world. Crossing international boundaries, they argue, is not an "alternative" to development; it is in fact one of the components of development, significantly raising the average income of the set of persons born in a specific country.

Despite the greater difficulty of collecting data that goes beyond the framework of national borders, placing internal and international migration within the same framework is a logical next step in examining such current topics as remittances, brain drains/gains, and the role of diaspora populations within overall human development strategies.[26]

Remittances

Since the World Bank's focus on the issue in *Global Economic Prospects 2006*, remittances have become part of the mainstream discussion on development. The most recent estimates from the World Bank (2010) note that recorded remittances to developing countries worldwide will recover to $325 billion in 2010, up from $307 billion in 2009, and may even exceed $370 billion by 2012. Despite declines due to the world economic crisis, remittances were more resilient than other financial flows, and remained almost three times greater than official development assistance (ODA) to developing countries.

Flows to Sub-Saharan Africa were estimated at a stable $21 billion a year from 2008 to 2010, and projected to increase to $24 billion in 2012. In contrast to the global picture, totals for recorded remittances to Africa were not greater than flows of ODA. According to the World Bank, the top five remittance-receiving countries were Nigeria ($10.0 billion), Sudan ($3.2 billion), Kenya ($1.8 billion), Senegal ($1.2 billion), and South Africa ($1.0 billion). In terms of remittances as a percentage of gross domestic product (GDP), the top five were Lesotho (24.8%), Togo (10.3%), Cape Verde (9.1%), Guinea-Bissau (9.1%), and Senegal (9.1%). In North Africa, grouped with the Middle East in World Bank data, the top remittance-receiving countries were Egypt ($7.7 billion), Morocco ($6.4 billion), Algeria ($2.0 billion), and Tunisia ($2,0 billion). As a percentage of GDP, remittances were highest in Morocco (6.6%), Tunisia (5.3%), Egypt (4.0%), and Algeria (1.4%).[27]

---

26. For an extensive review of current policy debates on these specific issues, and more current statistics, published too late to the new data be incorporated systematically into this essay, see Ratha et al. (2011).
27. But, notes the World Bank (2009a: 8), remittance data for Sub-Saharan Africa is thought to be even less reliable than in other world regions. Flows are probably substantially higher than reported.

There is a growing consensus in current research and policy debate that remittances should not be seen as substitutes for other sources of national financing, such as development assistance or foreign investment. Their economic contribution, channelled principally to direct family needs, is valuable in its own right, not only for the individuals and households receiving it but for national economies. As part of their mixed strategies for survival and advancement, households often combine international remittances with those from family members working in urban areas in the home country.[28] It follows that attempts to tax remittances or to channel them into development projects are likely to be less effective, from a national development standpoint, than helping households access and invest these remittances for their own survival and betterment, including in health and education.

The costs of sending remittances, which go principally through money transfer operators rather than through the banking system, are high. Although transmission costs have decreased somewhat worldwide, from 9.8% for a $200 transfer in last quarter of 2008 to 8.9% in the first quarter of 2010, the reduction was principally in the U.S./Mexico corridor, with rates remaining high in Africa.[29] Substantial savings could be achieved by introducing greater competition into the system, and a Global Remittances Working Group initiated by the G8 countries in 2008 has called for reducing the cost by 5 percentage points over five years. By requiring providers of remittance services to be more transparent about fees, the Wall Street Reform and Consumer Protection Act, signed into U.S. law in 2010, has the potential to give greater leverage to remitters. But the global remittance market is still dominated by large players such as Western Union and MoneyGram, which face little competition in many smaller markets.

While greater competition may bring about incremental reductions in remittance costs, the extent of competition also depends on the size of the national markets and the extent of government initiatives specifically aimed at promoting lower costs. According to the World Bank, Sub-Saharan Africa has the highest average cost among regions, at 11.57% in the third quarter of 2010.

A promising advance in some African countries is the introduction of money transfer via mobile phone, beginning with M-Pesa in Kenya. This trend is likely to continue. But it has as yet had little impact on transfers across national borders. If regulatory barriers could be overcome, this technology could have a very substantial competitive impact on lowering international remittance costs as well, particularly between neighbouring countries within Africa.

With continued emphasis from the World Bank and related agencies, remit-

---

28. See, for example, the study of Ghanaian migrant networks by Valentina Mazzucato, in DeWind and Holdaway 2008: 71-102.
29. For regularly updated data, see the World Bank's database on remittance prices (http://remittanceprices.worldbank.org/).

tances are likely to receive sustained policy attention. However, it is still important to contextualize these financial flows with respect to other flows, in order to evaluate their potential impact on development. These other flows include not only foreign investment, official development assistance, and trade balances, but also the very substantial illicit financial flows, which are even less well tracked than remittances and only now beginning to attract more systematic international attention.[30]

The reforms needed for accurate reporting of data of illicit financial flow are daunting. They include transparency on country-by-country accounts of multinational corporations, documentation of the true residence of beneficiaries of banking accounts, and exchange of tax information between governments in the case of suspicious transactions. In contrast to remittances, however, the amounts involved in individual transactions are likely to be substantial. In looking at the results for inequality within and between countries, and among those born in a country (including diasporas), such flows should also become an essential part of the migration and development debate.

Brain Drains and Gains

The "brain drain," or loss of skilled workers through emigration, has long been the subject of policy debate and development research. It has also received significant attention in the media. The migration of health workers is particularly visible, with large numbers of foreign doctors and nurses working in developed countries while health crises grip African and other developing countries.[31]

Nevertheless, despite a significant body of research, reliable data are elusive, and effective solutions even more so.[32] For Africa, where the total rate of emigration was 1.8% in 2000, the rate of emigration of high-skilled workers was more than five times greater, at 10.4% (Marfouk 2007: 17). Twenty-five African countries had high-skilled emigration rates of 15% or more. The top ten were Cape Verde (67%), The Gambia (63%), Mauritius (56%), Seychelles (56%), Sierra Leone (53%), Ghana (47%), Mozambique (45%), Liberia (45%), Kenya (38%), and Uganda (36%). The largest absolute number of high-skilled emigrants came

---

30. In recent studies, Global Financial Integrity (http://www.gfif.org) has begun efforts to estimate these flows. According to this nongovernmental organization, illicit capital flows worldwide from crime, corruption, and trade mispricing amounted to some $1.26 trillion in 2008, having increased by 18% a year since 2000 from a base figure of $369.3 billion. Illicit financial flows out of Africa were estimated at at $63.8 billion in 2008, including some $37 billion from Nigeria alone (Global Financial Integrity 2010, 2011).
31. For recent sources on health worker migration see http://www.guardian.co.uk/global-health-workers, http://www.who.int/hrh/migration/en, and http://www.who.int/workforcealliance/en/.
32. For data sources, see particularly Docquier (2007), Docquier and Marfouk (2006), and the online datasets at http://perso.uclouvain.be/frederic.docquier/oxlight.htm. Summary statistics for African skilled migration, as of 2000, are in Marfouk (2007).

from countries with larger populations, including South Africa (168,000), Nigeria (149,000), Egypt (149,000), Morocco (141,000), and Algeria (86,000).

The losses to sending countries from emigration of skilled emigrants, particularly in the cases of smaller and least developed countries, are clear. In recent years, some scholars have also pointed to "brain gain" effects, such as remittances, return migration of migrants with added skills, diaspora contributions to development, and the effect of the opportunity for overseas education and employment in increasing incentives for professional education in sending countries. It is generally agreed, however, that these positive effects are unlikely to be sufficient to compensate for negative effects in most developing countries.[33]

The most extensive policy debate on skilled migration has dealt with health workers. However, there is now a growing consensus that the principal responses to date have been ineffective.[34] These include measures to prohibit migration of skilled workers (not only ineffective but also in violation of the rights of migrants themselves) or to pay incentives for return (of limited effectiveness). Most widely discussed has been the development of voluntary codes of conduct, culminating in the World Health Assembly's adoption of the "WHO Global Code of Practice on the International Recruitment of Health Personnel" (WHA63.16, 21 May 2010).

Even when voluntary codes are adopted, however, they face a policy climate in developed countries which systematically encourages the immigration of skilled labour. Moreover, professionals continue to be attracted by the higher salaries and generally better working conditions in the rich countries. In the health field, it is unlikely that brain drain issues can be addressed effectively without broad international cooperation to reduce inequality in health systems and health outcomes between countries. The shortage of health personnel in developed as well as developing countries needs to be met through an expansion of education and training capacity, both overall and in the most disadvantaged countries in particular. Global health budgets need to be provided with sustainable financing from both national and international sources, including new innovative financing mechanisms such as those being developed by UNITAID.

In short, the perspective needs to shift to the development of health systems rather than focusing only on the migration of health workers. The supply of health workers is just one of multiple factors affecting health systems equity. Promoting quality health systems both requires and attracts skilled health professionals. If that is accepted as the shared goal, both at national and international levels and by health institutions and professionals themselves, then distribution

---

33. See Docquier (2007) and several chapters in Özden and Schiff (2006).
34. See, in particular, Physicians for Human Rights (2004), Mensah, Mackintosh, and Henry (2005), and Khadria (2010).

of personnel to meet the needs can be addressed—not only by encouraging return of skilled professionals to their countries of origin, but also by more flexible forms of temporary assignment and collaboration across national lines.

International coordination in planning for human resources in health, including these and other measures, has recently taken significant steps forward with the first Global Forum on Human Resources for Health, held in 2008 in Kampala, Uganda, and the second, which took place in Bangkok, Thailand, in January 2011. The forums are managed by a multi-stakeholder Global Health Workforce Alliance (http://www.who.int/workforcealliance/en/). They aim to address the worldwide shortage of health workers, estimated at 4.2 million, with 1.5 million needed in Africa alone. The Alliance has identified 57 countries that urgently need additional human resources to meet health crises, of which 39 are in Africa.

African Union Draft Strategic Framework on Migration in Africa: Suggested Actions on Brain Drain

- Counter the exodus of skilled nationals by promoting the NEPAD strategy for retention of Africa's human capacities; targeting economic development programmes to provide gainful employment, professional development and educational opportunities to qualified nationals in their home countries.
- Counter the effects of "brain drain" by encouraging nationals abroad to contribute to the development of their country of origin through financial and human capital transfers such as short and long term return migration, the transfer of skills, knowledge and technology including in the context of programmes such as the IOM MIDA (Migration in Development for Africa) Programme, and activities of ILO, WHO and other relevant agencies.
- Foster private sector opportunities to provide alternative employment to the low paying public sector and reduce brain drain
- Member States establish policies for the replacement of qualified persons who have left the country of origin and implement retention policies and related strategies.
- Maximize the contribution of skilled professionals in the continent by facilitating mobility and deployment of professionals in a continental and regional framework

African Union (2005: 27)

In other areas of the economy, as in health, actions on brain drain should not be aimed at reducing mobility but rather at flexibly integrating professional development and employment within broader development strategies. Consensus around goals such as those laid out by the African Union (see box) is growing. The UNDP's TOKTEN (Transfer of Knowledge through Expatriate Nationals) program, established in 1977, is being joined by a host of parallel efforts, such as the World Bank's African Diaspora Program. Their success, however, is likely to depend primarily on the progress of development in specific sectors and specific countries.[35]

Diasporas and Development

While policy debates on the specific topics of remittances and brain drain are most advanced, there is also growing interest in the overall role of diasporas in development. Topics include the role of migrant organizations in "co-development" projects, investment of capital from the diaspora both directly and through mechanisms such as "diaspora bonds," and, more generally, the need for governments to create structures to actively involve emigrant communities in national development. Given the heterogeneity of diasporas and country situations, however, the development of general lessons has been limited and is likely to remain so.[36]

The priorities for governments and agencies in countries of origin and in host countries should be to recognize the diversity of diaspora-initiated activities under way and selectively foster those with the greatest benefits for development, rather than attempting to bring them all under one umbrella. Examples of African countries which have taken significant steps in this direction are Morocco and Cape Verde. Mali has established a Ministry for Malians Abroad and African Integration; it also provides representation for Malians abroad in government institutions, and allows dual citizenship.[37] In the Moroccan diaspora the nongovernmental organization Migrations et Développement has established a solid track record of accomplishment (Ould Aoudia 2010). AFFORD UK (http://www.afford-uk.org) has worked for more than a decade to encourage involvement of Africans in the United Kingdom in development on the African continent, and the Eunomad networks (http://www.eunomad.org), founded in 2007, are now functional in nine European countries. There are a host of both formal and informal diaspora organizations for almost every country, at multiple levels.[38] But most are documented only sporadically. Unlike the topic of

---

35. Among the most promising, which can be implemented at multiple levels, are programs for collaboration between universities. See, for recent reports, focused on Europe and Africa in particular, the program co-sponsored by the European University Association, the Association of African Universities, and related groups (http://www.accesstosuccess-africa.eu).
36. For a clear analysis, see de Haas (2006a). Other recent reviews of the literature include Agunias (2009), Pastore (2007), and Ionescu (2006). Eunomad (2010) provides a review of practices of co-development in 9 European countriees.
37. For more examples of African government diaspora programs, see Ratha et al. (2011: 177–179.)
38. As one example, see the Eko Club International network of Lagosians in the diaspora, with chapters in North America and Europe which support medical and educational projects in Lagos (http://ekoklubinternational.com).

remittances, the impact of diaspora organizations is one on which there is still very little systematic data.

There is little doubt that "migration and development" is well on the way to becoming an established item on the development agenda and in negotiations between countries of origin and destination. But, except in the specific areas of remittances and brain drain, the prospects for new policy developments still seem limited. Scholars and many officials recognize the self-defeating danger in linking development aid to pressure for more restrictions on migration, and the folly of assuming that development will reduce migration. Yet such perspectives are strongly entrenched. And development policies involving diasporas are subject to the same constraints as development policies more generally. Just as the prospects for development depend on the wider political context in both developing and developed countries, the potential role of diasporas depends on where they are placed with respect to the political and economic structures in both societies.

For example, options such as voting abroad and dual citizenship have been applauded as increasing the opportunities for continued diaspora involvement in countries such as Ghana, yet they are inextricably entangled with political divisions in most national contexts in Africa. The multiple roles of the diaspora are certainly significant in cases such as Zimbabwe, Eritrea, or Nigeria, for example. But the options for their involvement in development depends above all on the broader political and social context of which they are a part. The nature of their involvement also depends on whether diaspora groups are committed to inequality-reducing development or are linked primarily to privileged class networks within their country of origin.

In destination countries, the option of adopting migration policies that contribute to human development is severely constrained by political realities. In its chapter laying out policies to "enhance human development outcomes" from migration, the 2009 Human Development Report (UNDP 2009: 95-112) includes "liberalizing and simplifying regular channels that allow people to seek work abroad." It cautiously suggests not only regularizing the status of irregular migrants but also expanding the number of visas for unskilled workers. The report also suggests, but does not fully elaborate, the concept of human development of peoples (UNDP 2009: 14; Ortega 2009), measuring human development not by country of current residence but by country of origin.

In these terms, as explained most fully by Lant Pritchett in *Let Their People Come* (Pritchett 2006), the most effective action developed countries could take for development would be to open their borders more widely, particularly for unskilled immigrants, who both gain substantially themselves by migration and are most likely to maintain family connections with those most in need in their countries of origin. The trend in immigration policy, however, is precisely the reverse: countries increasingly favour skilled migrants. Pritchett proposes expanding strictly defined temporary contract migration, as in the Gulf Co-operation Council states, to counter policy opposition to such measures. But that begs the question of the difficulty of protecting the rights of migrants and increasing inequality within destination states. The political feasibility of these or other measures for regularizing and expanding mobility to promote development will depend, it is clear, on fundamental changes in public understandings of both the rights of migrants and the right to migrate. That is the subject of the next section of this essay.

MIGRATION AND HUMAN RIGHTS

As noted above, in the section on East and Central Africa, even in the case of refugees, those migrants with rights most clearly defined by international agreements, implementation of those rights is highly inconsistent. In some cases, such as the "warehousing" of refugees in long-term camps, such violations are institutionalized and hardly noted. Similarly, the rights of migrants more generally, even when established by international or national law, are often ignored in practice and have little public recognition. The legitimacy of a hierarchical rights regime, privileging first citizens, then residents with regular documentation, and last of all irregular migrants, is rarely questioned. In recent years, notes the UN's Special Rapporteur on the Human Rights of Migrants (UN 2010), the trend towards "criminalization of migration" has led to increasing abuses of human rights.

The gap between stated principles and practice, together with the relatively low level of international attention given to violation of migrants' rights, make it important not only to consider the legal frameworks in place but also the underlying assumptions and climate of opinion that affect the prospects for change. This section first considers the Convention of the Rights of Migrants, which entered into force in 2003 but which almost no major immigrant-receiving country has adopted. This is followed by a brief discussion of universal human rights instruments that, for the most part, apply to migrants as well as citizens of a country, of the threats posed by anti-immigrant sentiment and xenophobic actions, and of the ambivalent character of government migration policies. Finally, this section looks at the less-well-defined issue of the right to migrate.

Convention on the Rights of Migrants

The United Nations Convention on the Protection of the Rights of All Migrant Workers and Members of Their Families (commonly referred to as the Convention on the Rights of Migrants) was approved by the United Nations General Assembly over two decades ago, in 1990. In 2003, it achieved the minimum number of ratifications to enter into force. But as of 2010, there were only 44 states that had become full parties to the convention, and 15 that had signed but not yet ratified it.

The 59 states include only 4 in Europe (all small Balkan states and no members of the European Union). Other major immigration countries, such as Canada, United States, Australia, and the Gulf Cooperation Council states, have also not signed. African states, but not including South Africa, Côte d'Ivoire, Kenya, or Tanzania, account for 27 of the 59 states; 14 are in West Africa, the region with the most open migration regime.[39] Among African states with a significant influx of migrants, Algeria, Egypt, Libya, and Morocco, all of which also have significant flows of emigration, are parties to the treaty. But it is not at all clear that these countries have considered it applicable to immigrants to their countries as well as their own emigrants.

In principle, the Convention does not establish new rights, but spells out in greater detail the procedures for ensuring basic human rights that are established for all by the International Covenants on Civil and Political Rights and on Economic, Social and Cultural Rights, and other core human rights treaties (UNDP 2009: 99–102; http://www2.ohchr.org/english/issues/migration/). The Convention, however, has stronger provisions for non-discrimination than other more general treaties, spelling out protections that apply to all migrant workers, independent of regular or irregular status, as well as additional rights that apply to migrant workers with regular status.

Such core human rights as the rights to life, to freedom of expression, to security of person and due process, and to education, for example, are not limited by migrant status (see statement by Global Migration Group in box below). The Convention spells out other rights as, for example, the right to consular representation, the right to equal access to participation in trade unions, and the right to emergency medical care. While the Convention does not explicitly guarantee the right to family unification, it does include a provision encouraging states to facilitate family unification.

In 1998 United Nations agencies, trade unions, migrants' organizations, and other civil society groups including Human Rights Watch and the World Council of Churches jointly launched a Global Campaign for Ratification of the Convention.[40] This campaign deserves support, not least as a vehicle for encouraging wider attention to migrants' rights. But, given that the majority of rights included are already mandated by other treaties or even by national law and, even so, are frequently violated, groups concerned with migrants' rights should give even greater priority to effective measures to defend those rights which are already established in principle.

Universal Human Rights

The Bill of Rights in the South African Constitution opens with the statement that it "enshrines the rights of all people in our country." In the following clauses, with the exception of rights specifically referring to citizens, such as section 19 on political rights, the rights included—ranging from the right to life and

---

39. For a current list of signatories, consult the UN treaty database at http://treaties.un.org. In Southern Africa only Lesotho is a party to the convention.
40. For more information on the ratification campaign, see http://www.december18.net and http://www.migrantrights.org.

the security of the person to adequate housing, health care, and education—are extended to "everyone." "Every worker" has the right to join a trade union. The application of many of these rights to non-citizens has been confirmed in a series of court cases (Manby 2009: 149).

Similarly, the core international human rights treaties include migrants. Article 1 of the Universal Declaration of Human Rights says that "All human beings are born free and equal in dignity and rights." Article 2 adds that "Everyone is entitled to all the rights and freedoms set forth in this Declaration, without distinction of any kind, such as race, colour, sex, language, religion, political or other opinion, national or social origin, property, birth or other status." The International Covenant on Civil and Political Rights and the International Covenant on Economic, Social and Cultural Rights contain similar language.

In South Africa, as likely in many other countries,[41] much of the public does not agree with these provisions, even if they are enshrined into law. In a 2006 survey (Crush 2008:28), for example, 29% of respondents said that migrants should not have the right to legal protection, 17% that they should not have the right to police protection, and 19% that they should not have access to social services. Even larger percentages (67% for legal protection, 65% for police protection, and 68% for access to social services) said that "illegal immigrants" should not have such rights.

As noted by the Global Migration Group[42] in a recent statement (see box), the protection of irregular migrants from rights abuses is a state responsibility which should not be trumped by other concerns. Yet such abuses worldwide are driven not only by anti-immigrant public opinion but also by the push by state authorities towards more restrictive immigration controls and what UN Special Rapporteur Jorge Bustamente terms the increasing "criminalization" of irregular migration (UN 2010). Undocumented migrants are widely stereotyped as potential criminals or terrorists. And through profiling the same stereotypes are applied as well to documented immigrants and ethnic groups associated with immigrant populations.

Elaborating the dangers of further criminalization of irregular migration, Bustamente's 2010 report notes that this trend, earlier identified in his 2008 report, continues. Human rights have not been integrated into migration management policies, which have overemphasized law enforcement measures. Criminal penalties for violations of immigration law, which are victimless crimes, are not

---

41. Despite the availability of some comparative public opinion data (see Crush and Ramachandran 2009: 7; Kleemans and Klugman 2009), the questions available in other countries are not as specific about rights as those in the South African survey.
42. The Global Migration Group earlier published a systematic report on the relationship between international migration and human rights (Global Migration Group 2008). See also Grant 2005.

Statement of the Global Migration Group* on the Human Rights of Migrants in Irregular Situation

[excerpts]

30 September 2010

* The Global Migration Group (GMG) is an inter-agency group bringing together 14 agencies (12 United Nations agencies, the World Bank, and the International Organization for Migration) to promote the application of relevant international instruments and norms relating to migration, and to encourage the adoption of more coherent, comprehensive and better coordinated approaches to the issue of international migration.

http://www.globalmigrationgroup.org

Migrants in an irregular situation are more likely to face discrimination, exclusion, exploitation and abuse at all stages of the migration process. ...

Too often, States have addressed irregular migration solely through the lens of sovereignty, border security or law enforcement, sometimes driven by hostile domestic constituencies. Although States have legitimate interests in securing their borders and exercising immigration controls, such concerns cannot, and indeed, as a matter of international law do not, trump the obligations of the State to respect the internationally guaranteed rights of all persons, to protect those rights against abuses, and to fulfil the rights necessary for them to enjoy a life of dignity and security.

The fundamental rights of all persons, regardless of their migration status, include:

- The right to life, liberty and security of the person and to be free from arbitrary arrest or detention, and the right to seek and enjoy asylum from persecution;
- The right to be free from discrimination based on race, sex, language, religion, national or social origin, or other status;
- The right to be protected from abuse and exploitation, to be free from slavery, and from involuntary servitude, and to be free from torture and from cruel, inhuman or degrading treatment or punishment;
- The right to a fair trial and to legal redress;
- The right to protection of economic, social and cultural rights, including the right to health, an adequate standard of living, social security, adequate housing, education, and just and favourable conditions of work.

...

Protecting these rights is not only a legal obligation; it is also a matter of public interest and intrinsically linked to human development.

...

The irregular situation which international migrants may find themselves in should not deprive them either of their humanity or of their rights. As the Universal Declaration of Human Rights states: "all human beings are born free and equal in dignity and rights"

only inappropriate. They are ineffective in making migration or the destination society more secure, and foster a climate conducive to human rights abuses. Immigration detention is particularly subject to such abuse, as is the use of deportation procedures which do not respect due process.

This emerging consensus among international agencies on the necessity to "mainstream" human rights standards into migration management is a welcome development. Implementation of such policies, however, will depend primarily on national and local efforts. Measures to counter anti-migrant opinion and actions are likely to be ineffective unless they go hand in hand with public advocacy for alternate inclusive views and policies.

Anti-Migrant Attitudes, Discrimination, and Violence

Despite rising attention in public debate and by researchers to anti-migrant attitudes, discrimination, and violence—in their extreme forms often labelled with the term "xenophobia"—there is little consensus on what are the most important causes or the most effective remedies. The term xenophobia itself, and other labels such as "exclusionary nationalism," do not have agreed definitions. Surveys designed to measure such attitudes use different questions, making comparisons difficult.[43]

Nevertheless, there are a number of general observations that seem justified by the evidence:

- World-wide anti-immigrant and anti-immigration attitudes are significant, but most generally in the minority. In the World Values survey for 2005/2006, for example, 20% of respondents said that ethnic diversity compromises a country's unity, about 25% said they would object to living next to a migrant. In the same survey, 11% said that people should be prohibited from coming as immigrants, while another 38% said there should be strict limits on immigration.
- Trends in recent years, with data available particularly for Western Europe, tend to show increasing or stable levels of hostile attitudes to immigrants, accompanied by more restrictive immigration policies (Ceobanau and Escandell 2010: 311–313). While there is no comparable comparative evidence available from other regions, anti-migrant attitudes and actions characterized as xenophobia have been noted from countries as varied as South Africa, India, Malaysia, Libya, and Thailand (Crush and Ramachandran 2009).
- The determinants of anti-immigrant attitudes are complex. Reviewing evidence on micro-level determinants, Ceobanu and Escandell (2010) cite find-

---

43. For a recent comprehensive survey of research on public attitudes on immigrants and immigration, see Ceobanu and Escandell (2010). The most extensive data available is for Western European countries. See also the wide array of survey questions in Transatlantic Trends (2010) which includes the United States, Canada, and six European countries.

ings suggesting individual-level links from lower education and labor-force status to more hostile attitudes,[44] as well as from perceptions of threat and from right-wing ideological views. At the level of contextual determinants, they cite the effects of economic conditions and of the visibility of an immigrant group in a particular area, connected not so much with size as with abrupt increases in immigration into the area.
- Whether or not anti-immigrant attitudes are also accompanied by systematic discrimination and/or outbreaks of overt violence depends largely on the cues given by national and local government officials and other political forces, as well as the media and civil society. National and local governments can contribute to such hostile attitudes and actions not only by instigating them but also by failure to anticipate, acknowledge, or take efforts to control them.
- Anti-immigrant attitudes and actions are rarely if ever directed against all immigrants as such, but differ significantly by other criteria, although such distinctions are only rarely incorporated in opinion surveys, particularly surveys with a cross-national scope. These include distinctions between regular and irregular immigrants, as well as between skilled and unskilled immigrants. They also track existing racial, ethnic, cultural, and religious hierarchies, both within-nation hierarchies and those associated with the histories of global inequality.

It is clear that how African immigrants fit with these intersections of race, religion, and internal ethnic divisions differs significantly not only by world region but by country, and, indeed, by local areas within countries. This requires nuanced exploration of particular national contexts, a task beyond the scope of this general review. One can note briefly, however, some elements which seem to be common to at least some multi-country groups.

In each context, African immigrants are commonly perceived within the context of stereotypes applicable to immigrants and minority ethnic groups more generally. Thus, in Western Europe, where most African migrants are from North Africa, stereotypes and discrimination are most often discussed in reference to the category of "Muslims," although, depending on the national context, Muslims may also include larger numbers of Turks or Pakistanis than North Africans. In the post-9/11 context, this religious identity is also associated with suspicions of Islamic extremism and terrorism, even though those involved are very small minorities among the Muslim population. For sub-Saharan African immigrants, anywhere in the world, race is both the dominant visible characteristic and the occasion for deep-rooted stereotypes and prejudices based on centuries

---

44. Ceobanu and Escandell's review, however, is almost entirely limited to developed countries. It does not consider evidence from South Africa, discussed above, which shows no or small differences for these social background variable.

of global racism. Some national groups, such as Somalis, have the distinction of being subject to both religious and racial grounds for discrimination.

But different national contexts shape the intersection of religion and race with immigrant status in very different ways. In the United States, the United Kingdom, and Canada, for example, sub-Saharan African immigrants are part of larger "black" populations, and that status is often more relevant to prejudice and discrimination against them than their immigrant status. But in the United States, anti-immigrant sentiment is linked primarily to the largest group of unskilled immigrants, those from Latin America. In both North America and Europe, Muslim citizens and immigrants form very internally diverse populations, but the "African" component of the Muslim population is prominent only in a few cases, such as North Africans in France or Somalis in both Europe and the United States.

Within Africa, in the very different contexts of Libya and South Africa, anti-immigrant attitudes and action particularly target black immigrants from other African countries, in contrast to those from other Arab countries (in Libya) or Western countries (in South Africa). Elsewhere on the continent, Zimbabwe has targeted both those of European descent and those with family origins in neighbouring African countries. In Côte d'Ivoire, immigrant status and Muslim identity have been conflated in internal conflicts. And in a much wider set of African countries, descent from "foreign" ancestors, even several generations back, has served to identify people for discrimination, denial of citizenship, or expulsion.

Both outside Africa and within the continent, one common thread underlying the diverse and changing environment for immigrants and descendants of immigrants is how national identities and policies on citizenship and immigration are shaped both as inclusive and exclusive. In every case, the issue is not only how those with extreme views think and act as individuals, but also how governments routinely handle the issues of rights with respect to immigrants.

Governments and Migrants' Rights

Both nationality and citizenship[45] imply exclusion as well as inclusion, simultaneously defining who is included and who is not. All nation-states today inherit complex amalgams of cultural and legal traditions defining these distinctions, based on the European "nation-state" concept and on the parallel evolution of "international" law.

Dating back to 19th century international debates, it is common to divide citizenship traditions into more exclusive ones based on the right of descent (*jus*

---

45. The two concepts are often used interchangeably, but here I distinguish nationality, referring to membership in a culturally defined "nation," and "citizenship," referring to membership defined by a state and conferring specific rights.

sanguinis), such as Germany, and those based on the right of birth in a country (*jus soli)*, such as France, as well as the countries of European migration overseas. That distinction is in turn correlated and thematically linked with contrasting concepts of nation-states as based on traditional cultural units or on voluntary allegiance to a state.

Particularly in the new environment of increasing diversity and volume of international migration, such a binary distinction is far too simple for characterizing the realities in any country, although some East Asian countries still come close to the more exclusive model. In countries receiving African migrants, both on and outside the African continent, the mix of inclusive and exclusive elements is both complicated and changing. These include not only how the nation and citizenship are defined, but also such other factors such as de facto differences of access to rights among nominal citizens of a given country, the ease of acquiring citizenship, and the extent to which rights of non-citizens, both regular and irregular immigrants, are recognized. The last element is becoming increasingly important due to new emphasis on the role of universal human rights (see previous section).[46]

In traditional countries of immigration, such as the United States, Canada, and Australia, the general principle of "birthright citizenship" is well-established, despite recent calls from right-wing Republicans in the United States for its abolishment. The incorporation of immigrants through naturalization, moreover, is a well-defined process that is also celebrated as part of national identities. Yet these countries also have strong exclusionary strains linked to histories of race and conquest, which until recent decades were also reflected in immigration legislation. In the United States, since 1965, visas for immigration are no longer allocated by national origins. Nevertheless, the legacy of slavery and more than a century of unequal rights among nominal citizens is still manifest in today's patterns of inequality. African immigrants thus enter a society of de facto unequal rights, remedies for which are impeded by U.S. refusal to accept the government's obligation to ensure equal social and economic as well as political rights. Attitudes and discriminatory actions applied to disadvantaged citizens, and mobilized by right-wing political groups, are easily transferred to immigrants, particularly unskilled immigrants who match the profiles of unfavoured minorities. Following 9/11, the creation of ICE (Immigration and Customs Enforcement) in 2003 marked a step-up not only of immigration enforcement but also its integration within a security framework. This highlighted the presumed

---

46. Particularly helpful summaries on general issues of citizenship and migration are Castles and Davidson (2000) and Castles and Miller (2009).

"threat" from immigrants and increased the scope for systematic human rights abuses (see box).[47]

> **ICE in the United States: Injustice for All Findings of the National Network for Immigrant and Refugee Rights**
> - DHS [Department of Homeland Security] is detaining and deporting immigrants at alarming rates; communities are devastated and ICE deportations impact communities and the economy.
> - ICE uses prolonged and indefinite detention and the threat of loss of life and freedom to coerce persons jailed for immigration status offences into waiving their due process rights and accept deportation.
> - ICE ACCESS programs and collaboration between local police and immigration officials rely heavily on racial profiling, undermining community safety, and make immigrants more vulnerable to abuse and exploitation.
> - ICE's new workplace policing strategy of auditing employment files, allowing employers to fire undocumented workers en masse, has deepened the economic and humanitarian crisis in communities, increasing labour rights violations and other abuse.
> - The unrelenting militarization of immigration control and border communities is deliberately causing migrant deaths and violates the rights of border communities.
> - Local, county and state anti-immigrant legislative, policy proposals and ordinances across the country fuel and condone hate violence against immigrants and propel police and government abuses with impunity.
> – National Network for Immigrant and Refugees Rights (2010: 2–3)

In the United States, the prospect for systematic reform is limited not only by the political power of anti-immigrant forces, but also by an inherent contradiction in most reform proposals, which combine promises of regularized status for a subset of irregular migrants with continued restrictions on immigration and pledges of even more strict enforcement against those violating new regulations. Since irregular migration is driven by more fundamental inequalities, such reforms help set the scene for repetition of the same pattern of abuses.

In Europe, despite the diversity of national heritages, a convergence in immigration policies is being driven by the European Union policy development process (Collett 2010). While anti-immigrant attitudes are expressed both at local and national levels[48]—to cite only the most recent and prominent, the French government's actions against the Roma and the anti-immigrant views in

---

47. Among recent reports documenting these abuses, see National Network for Immigrant and Refugee Rights (2010). See also the websites of the American Civil Liberties Union, Amnesty International, and Human Rights Watch, which also monitor these issues.
48. See European Race Audit (2010a) for a review of local initiatives by extreme-right groups.

a new book by German banker Thilo Sarrazin—there is a similar contradiction within the EU policy structure itself. On the one hand, there are programs for "integration" of immigrant communities and human rights guidelines, monitored by the new Agency for Fundamental Rights (http://www.fra.europa.eu). On the other hand, Europe's FRONTEX, formed in 2006, works with national governments to implement active programs for deportation, more rigorous monitoring of borders, and stopping immigrants before arrival, whether at sea or through cooperation with transit and origin countries.[49]

In short, inclusion and exclusion are simultaneous realities. Flourishing immigrant communities, including African immigrants, are well-established in the developed countries of North America and Europe. Acknowledgement of multicultural realities is common currency in Europe as well as in traditional countries of immigration. But at the same time, governments, with support from strong sectors of public opinion, are also moving ahead with more and more elaborate policies of restrictive entry and deportations.

The structural obstacles to reform that respects migrants' rights, particularly the rights of irregular migrants, go far beyond the existence of far-right anti-immigrant parties and public sentiment. Security fears and security bureaucracies in the post-9/11 era foster a climate which excuses the violation of human rights. Politicians across the political spectrum cater to anti-immigrant sentiment, and anti-Islamic views have broad exposure in public debate (Hockenos, 2011). Efforts to protect irregular migrants must face the political reality that employers of irregular migrants profit from their vulnerability, which both sets up powerful political resistance to meaningful reform and undermines enforcement of those protections that do become law.

Nor, in most cases, can migrants in developed countries, particularly irregular or unskilled migrants, expect protection from their countries of origin. Despite the recent increase of interest in migration and development, the negotiations between countries of origin and destination have rarely incorporated representation of migrants themselves. Even when agreements do not negatively affect migrants, such as agreements on receiving deportees or cooperation in interception of migrants, the focus is most often narrowly on trade-offs of aid unrelated to migrant welfare or on macroeconomic financial gains from remittances and potential investments.

As outlined above in the section on the diversity of African migration, even such a general summary would be impossible for the range of migration situations within the continent.[50] Among African countries, South Africa and Libya

---

49. For a systematic review of deportation programs, see European Race Audit (2010b).
50. For a detailed overview of citizenship rights in Africa, see Manby 2009. Ongoing coverage of these issues is provided by the Citizenship Rights in Africa Initiative (http://www.citizenshiprights.org).

have certain parallels to the developed countries, in that immigration is driven largely by economic disparities with sending countries, and that black immigrants are those who particularly face the threat of xenophobia. But in other respects they differ profoundly. South African migration and human rights law is largely conducive to the protection of migrants' rights, although societal inequalities and public opinion push practice in exclusive directions. Libyan law and practice make citizenship rights inaccessible to any except descendants of Libyan citizens and, exceptionally, to those from other Arab states. And the authoritarian state has blocked protest and monitoring of human rights abuses, leaving few channels for protection of migrants' rights.

In some countries elsewhere on the continent migration and citizenship rights are closely linked to internal political conflict. The policies of most African countries in linking citizenship rights to descent rather than to birth create the potential for such linkages whenever there are large migrant flows. In 2011, these issues remain at the heart of conflicts in Côte d'Ivoire and the eastern Democratic Republic of the Congo. And they are among the most sensitive issues as Sudan sorts out the relationship between the soon-to-be South Sudan and the remainder of the country. As of early 2011, negotiations are still ongoing on definition of the status for Southerners in the North and Northerners in the South. But both the existing Sudanese constitution and draft constitutional proposals from South Sudan link citizenship to descent rather than to birth, one indicator pointing to the likelihood of serious disputes as millions of Sudanese suddenly become "migrants" in one of the two successor states (Assal 2011; Manby 2011).

Free Movement of Persons: The Right to Migrate

Thus, both in Africa and beyond, as outlined in the preceding pages, efforts to protect migrants' rights already promised in international law continue to face strong structural obstacles. Yet some voices are also beginning to raise other fundamental questions as well.

Should the authority granted to states to control migration itself be questioned, given its role in preventing human beings from seeking the protection of their fundamental rights by migrating?

Given the degree of regional and global integration, and the increasing freedom of movement of capital, goods, and services in an unequal world, must not human beings themselves also be guaranteed freedom of movement, however utopian such a proposal might seem to be? Isn't freedom of movement among the global public goods which should be the common heritage of the human family?

The prospect that states will in the foreseeable future relinquish their rights to control movement of persons is, of course, remote. But there is increasingly active debate, both on the ethical justification for freedom of movement and on the practical options for gradually expanding its scope. Two strands of this debate have significant relevance for African immigration. Most immediately there is the expansion of freedom of movement within African "regional economic communities."[51] Also relevant, although the debate on this is just beginning, is the obligation of rich countries to liberalize immigration from developing countries, in parallel with the broader obligation to provide their fair share of support for global human development.

Freedom of movement of persons within the African continent, long a Pan-African aspiration, was established as a goal in the Abuja Treaty of 1991, as part of the long-term plan for an African Economic Community. To date, however, what progress has been made has focused at the level of regional economic communities. As noted above in the section on West Africa, it is ECOWAS which has taken the most significant steps to implement this goal. More recently, the East African Community, reconstituted in 2000, established a common market in 2010, with provision for progressive implementation of "(i) free movement of goods; (ii) free movement of persons; (iii) free movement of workers; (iv) the right of establishment; (v) the right of residence; (vi) free movement of services; and (vii) free movement of capital." The East African Community, in contrast to its pre-1977 predecessor organization, since 2007 includes Rwanda and Burundi as well as the original members, Kenya, Tanzania, and Uganda.

In Southern Africa, the pace has been slow, and marked by strong disagreements among member states. This has resulted in a draft protocol on "facilitation" rather than "freedom" of movement, as well as limited progress on facilitation of movement through bilateral treaties. However, South Africa, Botswana, and Namibia—all countries attracting immigrants—continue to oppose full freedom of movement. Similarly, the broader Common Market for Eastern and Southern Africa, with 19 member states from Egypt to Swaziland, adopted a protocol including the free movement of persons. But implementation of that protocol has been patchy at best, with emphasis on freedom of trade rather than freedom of persons.

In more general terms, and particularly with respect to the right of movement from poor countries to rich countries, an increasing number of policy analysts and scholars are challenging the conventional acceptance of the sovereign right of states to deny entry to their borders. As noted above in the section on inequality, economist Branko Milanovic and sociologists Roberto Korzeniewicz and Timothy Moran have highlighted the consequences of widening global inequality and the injustice of determining life chances by the fate of a child's

---

51. For contrasting case studies of West Africa and Southern Africa, see the relevant chapters in Pécoud and de Guchteneire (2007). See also the website of the Institute for African Integration (http://iaiafrica.org).

citizenship. As noted in the section on migration and development, economist Lant Pritchett laid out the development benefits of expanding immigration of unskilled workers to developed countries.

Migration analysts and legal scholars have also begun to address related issues. A set of studies for the Global Commission on International Migration explored the option of what they called "Migration without Borders" (Pécoud and de Guchteneire 2005, 2007). The right to leave a country included in international human rights instruments, they argue, is incomplete if there is no comparable right to enter another country. And, they note, the strict limitation of immigration by sovereign nation-states should not be sacrosanct, and indeed was rarely consistently implemented prior to the 20th century.

International legal scholar Joel Trachtman (2009) systematically explores the case and the practical options for the "fourth freedom" of movement of labour (the first three being goods, services, and money). And legal philosopher Ayelet Shachar (2009) analyses the "birthright lottery" of allocation of citizenship rights (whether by descent or by birth) as establishing inequality by inheritance, similar to inheritance of property. Neither scholar advocates the full abolition of borders, but both argue that the inequality determined by the country of citizenship is unjust and that remedies must be found to address it.

Although recognizing the political obstacles to such measures, Trachtman argues for multilateral agreements expanding the prospects for increased migration, primarily benefiting migrants but also crafted, including adjustment mechanisms, so as to avoid losses to sending or receiving states or to particular disadvantaged groups. Shachar, in contrast, argues that open-admissions policies cannot be the sole or primary remedy. Instead, she presents the case for redistribution of resources through a "birthright privilege levy." Such a levy would be designed to ameliorate the inequalities due to the disparity of wealth by country of birth, while a new *jus nexi* (law of connection) could be developed as an alternative concept for opening citizenship more widely without full abolition of borders and devaluing membership in national communities.

It is no doubt true that opening the doors wider for non-skilled migrants to rich countries is an even more difficult goal than that of extending effective human rights protection to those migrants already resident or likely to move under current restrictions. But it is also an issue that will not go away, as long as large gaps in human development provide powerful incentives to move.

VARIETIES OF MIGRANTS' RIGHTS ORGANIZING

Like all immigrants, African immigrants in different countries have established a wide array of informal and formal organizations and networks for mutual assistance with practical issues, preservation of their culture, and advocacy for their interests. In many cases, human rights and other civil society groups in destination countries have also focused on these issues. Surveying these groups would be far beyond the scope of this essay, even if sufficient systematic data were available. Nevertheless, a few examples can illustrate some of the varieties of organizing efforts in particular.

Beginning with the classic manifesto of the Sans-Papiers of France, this section also presents brief descriptions of an activist non-governmental organization in California, of the response of the South African Congress of Trade Unions to the outbreak of xenophobic violence in South Africa in 2008, and of a report by the Migrants' Rights Network on local immigration policies in London, England.

Manifesto of the Sans-Papiers

In August of 1996, the "Sans-Papiers" ("Undocumented") of France gained international recognition when some 300 undocumented African women, children, and men were evicted by police from St. Bernard Church in Paris, where they had taken sanctuary to demand the regularization of their status. Since then the "Sans-Papiers" have become a movement with a presence around the country, winning some partial victories although their full objectives remain unrealized. The manifesto from 1997 is an eloquent statement of their case.

We Sans-Papiers of France, have decided, in signing this call, to come out of the shadows. Now, despite the risks involved, it is not only our faces but our names that are known. We proclaim:

As all undocumented immigrants, we are people like everyone else. We live among you, most of us for years. We came to France with the will to work and because we were told it was the "homeland of human rights." We could no longer endure the misery and oppression that was rampant in our countries, we wanted our children to have full stomachs and we dreamed of freedom. Most of us entered French territory through regular procedures. We have been arbitrarily thrown into illegality by the tightening of laws that allowed authorities not to renew our residence permits and by restrictions on the right of asylum, which has been reduced to a trickle. We pay our taxes, our rent, our living expenses … and our social security contributions when we can work regularly! When we are not subjected to unemployment and insecurity, we work hard in the garment, leather, construction, catering, and cleaning industries …

We experience the working conditions imposed on us by businesses and that you can reject more easily than we, as being undocumented makes us without rights. We know that this suits many people. We produce the wealth of France and we enrich France with our diversity. Sometimes we are single people who support our families at home. But we are also often here with our spouses and our children born in France or here from toddlers. We have given many of these children French names, we send them to school in the Republic. We have opened the path that should lead to the acquisition of French nationality, just as many French citizens, among the most proud to hold it, whose parents or grandparents were born abroad. In France we have our families, but also our friends.

We ask for papers to avoid being victims of arbitrary action by government, employers, and landlords. We call for papers so that we are no longer exposed to blackmail and betrayal. We call for papers to no longer suffer the humiliation of racial profiling, detention, deportations, the breakup of our families, and the perpetual fear. The Prime Minister of France promised that families would not be separated: we demand that this promise be finally met and that the repeated expression of the principles of humanity by the government be implemented. We ask for compliance with European and international conventions subscribed to by the French Republic. We count on the support of many French citizens, whose liberties could be threatened if our rights continue to be ignored. Since examples from Italy, Spain, Portugal, and on several occasions, France itself, demonstrate that general regularization of status is possible, we demand our regularization. We are not clandestine. We are here in the light of day. "

Source: Published in the supplement "55,000 names against the Debré law," *Libération*, February 25, 1997; translated from the French text at http://www.bok.net/pajol/film.html)

For more information: http://pajol.eu.org; http://9emecollectif.net; Raissiguier 2010.

Black Alliance for Just Immigration (BAJI)

Among immigrants to the United States, those born in Africa are a relatively small but rapidly growing portion. At some 1.4 million in 2007 (3.7% of the foreign-born population), most African immigrants have arrived since 1990, when there were only 364,000. The top five countries of origin were Nigeria, Egypt, Ethiopia, Ghana, and Kenya (Terrazas 2009). The majority of Immigrants from sub-Saharan Africa (some 1.1 million) find themselves both part of and distinct from native-born black Americans, while it is Hispanics who are the predominant immigrant group. Among the groups building progressive coalitions on this complex social terrain is the Black Alliance for Just Immigration, founded in 2006.

The mission of the Black Alliance for Just Immigration is to engage African Americans and other communities in a dialogue that leads to actions that challenge U.S. immigration policy and the underlying issues of race, racism and economic inequity that frame it.

BAJI's goal is to develop a core group of African Americans who are prepared to actively support immigrant rights and to build coalitions with immigrant communities and immigrant rights organizations to further the mutual cause of economic and social justice for all.

BAJI members are united on four principles:
- All people, regardless of immigration status, country of origin, race, colour, creed, gender, sexual orientation or HIV status deserve human rights as well as social and economic justice.
- Historically and currently, U.S. immigration policy has been infused with racism, enforcing unequal and punitive standards for immigrants of colour.
- Immigration to the United States is driven by an unjust international economic system that deprives people of the ability to earn a living and raise their families in their home countries. Through international trade, lending, aid and investment policies, the United States government and corporations are the main promoters and beneficiaries of this unjust economic system.
- African Americans, with our history of being economically exploited, marginalized and discriminated against, have much in common with people of colour who migrate to the United States, documented and undocumented.

BAJI supports an immigration policy with the following features:
- A fair path to legalization and citizenship for undocumented immigrants;
- No criminalization of undocumented workers immigrants or their families, friends and service providers;
- Due process, access to the courts and meaningful judicial review for immigrants;
- No mass deportations, indefinite detentions or expansion of mandatory detentions of undocumented immigrants;
- The strengthening and enforcement of labour law protections for all workers, native and foreign born;
- Reunification of families;
- No use of local or state government agencies in the enforcement of immigration laws.

BAJI is an education and advocacy group comprised of African Americans and black immigrants from Africa, Latin American and the Caribbean. It was founded in April 2006 in response to the massive outpouring of opposition of immigrants and their supporters to the repressive immigration bills then under consideration by the U.S. Congress.

Black activists in the Oakland/San Francisco Bay Area were called to action by Rev. Kelvin Sauls, a South African immigrant and Rev. Phillip Lawson, a long time Civil Rights leader and co-founder/co-chair of the California Interfaith Coalition for Immigrant Rights. BAJI also grew out of the efforts of the Priority Africa Network. PAN organizes Africa Diaspora Dialogues which have brought African Americans and black immigrants from Africa, the Caribbean and Latin America together to dialogue about the myths and stereotypes as well as the cultural, social and political issues that divide our communities.

Source: http://www.blackalliance.org

Congress of South African Trade Unions (COSATU)

Given the perception that immigrants compete for jobs with South African workers, the role of South Africa's strong trade union movement is particularly important. In a 2009 report on the response of South African civil society response to xenophobia, Strategy and Tactics researchers found a mixed response among unions.

COSATU has a long history of organising workers, including migrant workers, particularly in the mining sector. The global recession resulted in job losses and worsening conditions of work leaving a large section of its constituency vulnerable and under the impression that migrants are responsible for low wages. COSATU played a more active and activist role than the ANC and the SACP in response to the xenophobic outbreak [in 2008]. COSATU was present and active in the civil society responses in Cape Town, Durban, East London and Johannesburg. It did not play a prominent activist role, but various affiliates undertook important interventions. COSATU officials attributed the low levels of violence in the workplace to their intervention.

Until September 2009 COSATU did not have a strategy for organising migrant workers. The 2009 September Congress resolution represented a departure from past COSATU positions on migrant workers. It identifies capitalist globalisation as the systemic root of xenophobia. It commits COSATU to organise migrant workers and calls for migrant workers to be covered by labour law. Prior to the xenophobic attacks and the September 2009 resolution, COSATU did not see migrants as an important component of the working class struggle that need to be organised in their own right.

Source: Strategy & Tactics 2009, Summary, 20-21

The detailed study, by Mondli Hlatshwayo, was based on 44 interviews with trade union leaders and migrant group representatives. During the 2008 outbreak of xenophobic violence, Hlatshwayo reports, COSATU unions participated in humanitarian relief efforts for displaced migrants and helped to avoid anti-migrant violence in workplaces. The National Union of Mine Workers (NUM), whose members and leadership include many workers born outside South Africa, convened meetings and successfully prevented the spread of violence to the mines. Other unions indicating that they included migrants among their members and spoke out against the violence included the South African Transport and Allied Workers' Union (SATAWU) and the South African Commercial, Catering and Allied Workers' Union (SACCAWU).

In May 2008 the COSATU central executive committee issued a statement opposing the violence, saying that:

> COSATU is disgusted and ashamed at the small minority amongst us who have brought the country's good name into disrepute, by attacking, raping, robbing and murdering fellow Africans. Accordingly COSATU is totally opposed to xenophobia, racism, tribalism, sexism, regionalism and chauvinism. The most potent weapon is our unity – the unity of the working class.

Nevertheless, Hlatshwayo concluded from the interviews, COSATU's participation in civil society and community organizing against xenophobia was weak, and there was almost no commitment by COSATU member unions to organizing migrants or educating their membership against xenophobia.

Source: Hlatshwayo 2009.

Principles for London's progressive stance on immigration

In a 2010 report, the Migrants' Rights Network (MRN) in the United Kingdom, a wide coalition of migrant community organizations, non-governmental organizations, trade unions, and statutory organizations, focused on the strategic importance of London, a "global city" in which fully a third of the population was born outside the United Kingdom. Noting that migration flows have diversified significantly beyond the Commonwealth and European Union, with some 23% coming from Africa, the MRN report cites more positive attitudes towards immigration and diversity than elsewhere in the country, and suggests that the city must take the lead in pushing for more progressive national policies.

This report would like to propose four principles to policy makers and advocates which should underpin the development of strategy around immigration in London.

1. London should lead the way on making a case for progressive policies on immigration in the UK

London is well-placed to make a strong case for more progressive policies towards migrants because it is disproportionately affected by the consequences of restrictive policies. We have seen how London is home to the majority of the irregular population in the UK. ... The wider acceptance of diversity and the relatively more positive attitude to immigration that is evident in London compared to the UK means that representative London voices should be leading the debate on progressive immigration policy and not just dealing with the consequences of restrictions. Some leading London figures have already spoken in support of more progressive policies. For example, the mayor of London and several London boroughs already support the Strangers into Citizens Campaign on regularisation of irregular migrants – in contrast with national Labour and Conservative party policies.

However, more can be done. ...

2. Problems in London's labour and housing markets cannot be solved through immigration restrictions

Some of the issues that affect migrants most adversely are common to all of London's residents, especially wages, working conditions and access to affordable housing. Restrictions on migrants have only made the situation worse. Tackling low wages, poor working conditions and unemployment require labour market regulation. The shortage of affordable housing should be addressed through a housing strategy. Restricting migrants' access to welfare and social housing has only compounded the deficiencies in the labour market by forcing migrants to work under poor conditions. Labour market regulations that create better job security and ensure a London living wage would benefit both migrant workers, settled residents and, potentially, those outside the labour market or unemployed.

3. Development of local immigration enforcement in London should be scrutinised

The establishment of local enforcement teams within the UK Border Agency (UKBA) presents new challenges to a wide range of people within London. By developing partnerships with local service providers, the UKBA is hoping to extend the reach of immigration enforcement. Employers have already been brought into enforcing immigration rules by being required to check the entitlement to work of employees. There are plans to give service providers, including local authorities, housing providers and health services, a much more active role in immigration enforcement.

Overall, it is a bad idea to ask actors beyond the UKBA to have a role in immigration enforcement. This results in a lack of clarity about the rules and entitlements afforded to different groups, potentially leading to disproportionate effects on sectors of the regular migrant and settled population, especially on members of ethnic minority groups. Furthermore, immigration enforcement can jeopardise the work of service providers. ...

4. London's migrant strategy should be informed by migrants
Finally, migrants and immigration should be a central part of the policies that are decided at the London level, and especially the strategic plans which are responsibility of the GLA. It is critical to involve migrants themselves in developing the city's policies on immigration. The LSMP has already set out an integration strategy for refugees in London and is working towards widening its strategy to include all migrants – a project under development during 2010. The structure of the LSMP provides an arena in which migrant organisations can have a role in influencing the policies that affect them. It also creates the possibility of a constructive dialogue between migrant organisations and service providers. To make the most of these opportunities migrant organisations in London will need to articulate and put forward their views in an effective manner. ...

Source: Migrants' Rights Network 2010.

For more information: http://www.migrantsrights.org.uk.

FRAMING ADVOCACY AGENDAS

This brief review of the wide range of issues connected with African migration is hardly sufficient for formulating comprehensive "conclusions." What this final section does is rather to lay out summary observations on framing advocacy agendas, as food for thought and debate. There is also an annex exploring implications of migration issues for rethinking broader development goals and measures of progress, stressing the necessity to consider transnational as well as national units for measuring the goals of human development.

Migrants' Rights in Destination and Transit Countries

- The prerequisite for strong advocacy on migrants' rights is leadership from migrants' groups themselves. Among the most impressive examples, now sustained for more than 15 years, is that of the "Sans-Papiers" ("Undocumented") in France, whose leadership and support have featured immigrants from many African countries.
- While most migrants' self-help groups organize in groups defined by national or sub-national identities, or by occupation, political impact depends on the capacity to build networks bringing together immigrants from multiple national origins, including both regular and irregular immigrants and skilled as well as unskilled.
- Political impact also requires alliances with non-migrant groups, including not only human rights groups and allied disadvantaged minority groups, but also trade unions, churches, service agencies, and political parties.
- Given the widespread perception (and occasional reality) of conflicts of interests with native-born unskilled workers, critical variables include the strength of trade unions and whether unions seek to organize and support migrants' rights or reinforce anti-migrant public opinion.
- The Global Campaign for Ratification of the Rights of Migrants (see the guide to ratification on http://www.migrantsrights.org) deserves support. But in most destination and transit countries, campaigns for publicizing and implementing rights already established by international human rights treaties, as well as those practical implementation of protections available under national law, should take priority.
- In actions to protect individual migrants, it makes sense to take advantage of whatever legal remedies might apply, including eligibility for refugee status or other grounds for legal residency. However, migrants' rights campaigns should avoid the danger of reinforcing distinctions or promoting stereotypes of irregular migrants, and should stress that basic human rights are due to all migrants, without distinction.

Immigration "Reform" and "Managed Migration"

- Well-organized large-scale regularization programs, providing clear paths to regular status for irregular migrants, can have significant advantages not only for migrants but also for destination states, by moving sectors of the immigrant community out of the shadows. Notable examples include several waves of regularization in Spain (Arango and Jachimowicz 2005). In many cases, however, political opposition is very substantial. Note, for example, the 2010 defeat of the U.S. Dream Act to provide regularization for irregular migrants brought to the U.S. as children, despite majority popular support for its passage.
- In achieving reform measures including such positive elements as regularization, political compromises are no doubt inevitable. However, the most common trade-off, of simultaneously stepping up enforcement and deportation measures against the remaining irregular migrant population, is both inconsistent with protection of migrants' rights and unsustainable, recreating in a relatively short time the situation reform was presumably intended to resolve.
- Far more promising as trade-offs to satisfy at least some opponents of regularization would be compensatory mechanisms to protect sectors and communities which might be disproportionate losers from migration. As compared to simply "education" about human rights and the generally positive impact of migration, such measures could establish procedures to aid vulnerable native-born workers in sectors affected by migrant competition and to provide subsidies for communities having particularly high burden of social services or other adjustments to large migrant inflows.
- One "solution" that should definitely be rejected as illusory is new programs of "temporary migration" on the model of the earlier bracero or guest workers programs in the United States and Europe, respectively, or the current programs in the Gulf Cooperation Council countries. Even when accompanied by nominal protection for workers' rights, these are an open invitation to abuses of migrants through increasing their vulnerability to pressures from employers and their identification as a class of migrants with fewer rights to protect themselves.
- Given that "reform" proposals or systems of "managed migration" have a systematic tendency to include a mixture of policy measures, some of which may increase the likelihood of abuses of migrants' rights, there is also a need for legislative measures, independent administrative and judicial procedures, and civil society monitoring efforts specifically designed to protect the human rights of migrants.

- Reforms must take into account not only the regularization and protection of rights of existing migrant populations, but also provide for adequate regular channels for new migrants. They must provide not only flexibility for "circular migration" between origin and destination countries and for temporary migration for study or work but also paths for establishing permanent residency and citizenship.
- Continuing large flows of irregular migration are likely signals not only that reforms are still needed in migration policy but also that the levels of inequality between origin and destination countries are unacceptably high and need to be addressed by bilateral and multilateral inequality-reducing measures that include but also go beyond migration policy.

Migration and Global Human Development

- The impact of migration on human development should be gauged not only by the positive or negative impacts on countries of origin, as is the most conventional practice, but also by impacts on migrants themselves, on the set of all those born in countries of origin (whether they move or stay), on destination countries, and on the progress of human development and the extent of inequality in its distribution for the entire human family.
- Human development outcomes should be measured not only by changes in the levels of desired resources (income, health, education) but also by their impact in reducing inequalities, both within and between countries. A migration pattern biased towards higher-skilled migrants coming from the privileged sector of a country of origin, for example, would likely increase inequality both within the country of origin and within the larger group of those born in the country of origin, thus negating much of the positive impact of migration.
- For countries of origin, the value of policies in specific areas discussed above (such as remittances, brain drain, and diaspora contributions through investment or co-development) should be evaluated taking the effects on inequality into account. Remittances from unskilled workers to their families may thus have greater value than similar sums to more privileged families. The impact of measures to address brain drain in health, education, and other fields will depend primarily on the impact of the policies being implemented to advance health and education. And the net impact of investment or co-development projects by diaspora groups can only be evaluated within the context of wider development strategies led by developmental (or not so developmental) states.
- In destination countries, the movement to defend and extend migrants' rights is inextricably linked to the fate of broader movements to extend social justice, reduce internal inequality, and build inclusive concepts of national identity. As with these broader movements, this requires not only combating right-

wing attitudes and campaigns but also building positive visions of change and progressive political coalitions with the capacity to implement them.
- In the context of an unequal world, increased opportunities for migration, i.e., increasing the extent of the right to move, provide one path for reducing inequality between countries and greater global inequality. However, the right to move should also be matched by the right to stay, i.e., it should be possible for people to obtain their universal human rights, including economic and social opportunities, without being forced to leave their place of birth. That implies that migrants' rights must be accompanied by other measures to advance equality of human development between migrant-sending and migrant-receiving countries, including changes in the global economic order and in global responsibility for provision of basic human development needs.
- Migrant populations can play strategic roles in building links between their countries of destination and countries of origin, and in constructing networks for global community across national boundaries. Their capacity to do so, however, depends on the extent to which they maintain strong ties to both destination and origin countries, are linked to other progressive forces in both destination and origin countries, and pursue agendas benefiting not only themselves but also wider objectives of social justice.

In short, the quest for full rights for migrants—itself a goal to which global society has no far made only nominal commitments—must also be part of multifaceted efforts to establish new global as well as national social contracts for the 21st century. African migrants, coming from the region still most disadvantaged by the present world order, have strategic roles to play in establishing such contracts. They are simultaneously involved on multiple fronts: in their countries of origin, at the level of African unity, and in the relationships of Africa with the increasingly wide array of other societies in which the African diaspora has established its presence.

REFERENCES: BOOKS, REPORTS, AND ARTICLES

Note: The majority of these sources are available on-line and can be located through a web search. * indicates full text available free online as of 2010.

* Access to Success, 2010, *Africa-Europe Higher Education Cooperation for Development. White Paper.* Brussels: European University Association.

* Adepoju, Aderanti, 2008, *Migration in Sub-Saharan Africa.* Uppsala: Nordic Africa Institute.

* African Union, 2005, *Draft Strategic Framework for a Policy on Migration in Africa.* Addis Ababa: African Union.

Agunias, Dovelyn Ranneig, ed, 2009, *Closing the Distance: How Governments Strengthen Ties with Their Diasporas.* Washington: Migration Policy Institute.

* Amnesty International, 2007, *China: Internal Migrants: Discrimination and abuse. The human cost of an economic 'miracle.'* London: Amnesty International.

* Amnesty International, 2010, *From Life without Peace to Peace without Life: The Treatment of Somali Refugees and Asylum-Seekers in Kenya.* London: Amnesty International.

* Anarfi, John, and Stephen Kwankye, 2003, *Migration from and to Ghana: A Background Paper.* Sussex: Development Research Centre on Migration, Globalisation & Poverty.

* Assal, Munzoul A. M., 2011, *Nationality and Citizenship Questions in Sudan after the Southern Sudan Referendum Vote.* Bergen, Norway: Chr. Michelsen Institute.

* Bakewell, Oliver, and Hein de Haas, 2007, "African Migrations: continuities, discontinuities and recent transformations," in *African Alternatives*, ed. Patrick Chabal, Ulf Engel, and Leo de Haan, 95–118. Leiden: Brill.

* Bakewell, Oliver, 2008, "'Keeping Them in Their Place': the ambivalent relationship between development and migration in Africa," *Third World Quarterly*, 29:7, 1341–1358.

* Bakewell, Oliver, 2009, *South-South Migration and Human Development: Reflections on African Experiences.* Human Development Research Paper 2009/7. New York: UNDP.

* Barbour, Brian, and Brian Gorlick, 2008, *Embracing the 'Responsibility to Protect': A Repertoire of Measures incuding Asylum for Potential Victims.* Geneva: UNCHR.

Batalha, Luís, and Jørgen Carling, 2008, *Transnational Archipelago: Perspectives on Cape Verdean Migration and Diaspora.* Amsterdam: Amsterdam University Press.

* Batalova, Jeanne, ed., 2008, *Immigration: Data Matters.* Washington: Migration Policy Institute and Population Reference Bureau.

Cabrera, Luis, 2010, *The Practice of Global Citizenship.* Cambridge, UK: Cambridge University Press.

Castles, Stephen, and Mark J. Miller, 2009, *The Age of Migration: International Population Movements in the Modern World (4th ed.).* New York: Guilford Press.

Ceobanu, Alin M., and Xavier Excandell, 2010, "Comparative Analyses of Public Attitudes Toward Immigrants and Immigration Using Multinational Survey Data: A Review of Theories and Research," 309–328 in *Annual Review of Sociology*. Palo Alto, CA: Annual Reviews.

* Chan, Kam Wing and Will Buckingham, 2008, "Is China Abolishing the Hukou System?," in *China Quarterly*. London: China Quarterly.

* Clemens, Michael and Lant Pritchett, 2008, *Income per Natural: Measuring Development as if People Mattered More Than Places*. Washington: Center for Global Development.

* Cohen, Roberta, 2010, *Reconciling Responsibility to Protect with IDP Protection*. Washington, DC: Brookings Institution.

Cohen, Roberta, and Francis M. Deng, 1998, *Masses in Flight: The Global Crisis of Internal Displacement*. Washington, DC: Brookings Institution Press.

* Collett, Elizabeth, 2010, *The European Union's Stockholm Program: Less Ambition on Immigration and Asylum, But More Detailed Plans*. Washington, DC: Migration Information Source.

* Conchiglia, Augusta, 2007, "La Côte d'Ivoire tente la réconciliation nationale: Rôle central de l'immigration," 16–17 in *Le Monde Diplomatique*, December. Paris: Le Monde Diplomatique.

* Crush, Jonathan, 2008, *The Perfect Storm: The Realities of Xenophobia in Contemporary South Africa (Migration Policy Series No. 50)*. Cape Town, South Africa and Kingston, Canada: Southern African Migration Project.

Crush, Jonathan, Alan Jeeves, and David Yudelman, 1991, *South Africa's Labor Empire: A History of Black Migrancy to the Gold Mines*. Boulder, CO: Westview Press.

* Crush, Jonathan, Vincent Williams, and Sally Peberdy, 2005, *Migration in Southern Africa: A paper prepared for the Policy Analysis and Research Programme of the Global Commission on International Migration*. Geneva: GCIM.

* Crush, Jonathan, and Sujata Ramachandran, 2009, *Xenophobia, International Migration and Human Development*. Human Development Research Paper 2009/47. New York: UNDP.

* de Haas, Hein, 2006a, *Engaging Diasporas: How governments and development agencies can support diaspora involvement in the develoopment of origin countries*. The Hague: Oxfam Novib.

* de Haas, Hein, 2006b, *Trans-Saharan Migration to North Africa and the EU: Historical Roots and Current Trends*. Washington: Migration Information Source.

* de Haas, Hein, 2007, "North African migration systems: evolution, transformations and development linkages," in Castles, S. and Delgado Wise, R. (eds.), *Migration and Development: Perspectives from the South*. Geneva: International Organization for Migration

* de Haas, Hein, 2008a, "The Myth of Invasion: The inconvenioent realities of African migration to Europe," *Third World Quarterly* 29(7): 1305–1322.

* de Haas, Hein, 2008b, *Irregular Migration from West Africa to the Maghreb and the European Union: A Review of Recent Trends*. Geneva: International Organization for Migration.
* de Haas, Hein, 2009, *Mobility and Human Development*. Human Development Research Report 2009/1. New York: UNDP.
* December 18, 2010, *Ratification of the UN Migrant Workers Convention in the European Union: Survey on the Positions of Governments and Civil Society Actors*. Bruseels: December 18.
* Development Research Centre (DRC) on Migration, Globalisation & Poverty, 2009, *Making Migration Work for Development*. Sussex: University of Sussex.
* DeWind, Josh, and Jennifer Holdaway, 2008, *Migration and Development Within and Across Borders: Research and Policy Perspectives on Internal and International Migration*. Geneva: International Organization for Migration and New York: Social Science Research Counci.
* Docquier, Frédéric, 2007, "Brain Drain and Inequality among Nations," Paper prepared for the EUDN-AFS conference on Migration and Development. Paris.
* Docquier, Frédéric, and Abdeslam Marfouk, 2006, "International Migration by Education Attainment, 1990–2000," 227–244 in Çağlar Özden and Maurice Schiff, eds., *International Migration, Remittances, and the Brain Drain*. Washington, DC: World Bank.
* Esipova, Nell, Antia Pugliese, Rajesh Srinivasan, and Julie Ray, 2010, "Developed Nations Attract Young vs. Educated Migrants," November 9. Washington, DC: Gallup.
* Eunomad, 2010, *Migrations and Development: European Guide to Practices*. Brussels: Eunomad.
* European Race Audit, 2010a, *Direct Democracy, Racism, and the Extreme Right*. London: Institute of Race Relations.
* European Race Audit, 2010b, *Accelerated Removals: A Study of the Human Cost of EU Deportation Policies, 2009–2010*. London: Institute of Race Relations.
* GCIM (Global Commission on International Migration), 2005, *Migration in an Interconnected World: New Directions for Action*. Geneva: GCIM.
* Gemenne, François, 2011, "Climate-induced population displacements in a 4° C+ World," in *Philosophical Transactions of the Royal Society, A*, 182–195. London: Royal Society Publishing.
* Global Financial Integrity, 2010, *Illicit Financial Flows from Africa: Hidden Resource for Development*. Washington, DC: Global Financial Integrity.
* Global Migration Group, 2008, *International Migration and Human Rights*. Geneva: Global Migration Group.
* Grant, Stefanie, 2005, *International Migration and Human Rights*. Geneva: Global Commission on International Migration.

Hassim, Shireen, Tawana Kupe, and Eric Worby (eds.), 2008, *Go Home or Die Here: Violence, Xenophobia and the Reinvention of Difference in South Africa*. Johannesburg: Wits University Press.

* Hlatshwayo, Mondli, 2009, *COSATU's Responses to Xenophobia*. Johannesburg: Strategy and Tactics.

* Hockenos, Paul, 2011 "Europe's Rising Islamophobia," *The Nation*, May 9, 2011.

* Human Rights Watch, 2009, *From Horror to Hopelessness: Kenya's Forgotten Somali Refugee Crisis*. New York: Human Rights Watch.

* HSRC (Human Sciences Research Council), 2008, *Citizenship, Violence and Xenophobia in South Africa: Perceptions from South African communities*. Pretoria: HSRC.

* Ionescu, Dina, 2006, *Engaging Diasporas as Development Partners for Home and Destination Countries: Challenges for Policymakers*. Geneva: International Organization for Migration.

* Khadria, Binod, 2010, *The Future of Health Worker Migration: Background Paper WMR 2010*. Geneva: International Organization for Migration.

* Kleemans, Marieke, and Jeni Klugman, 2009, *Understanding Attitudes Towards Migrants: A Broader Perspective*. Human Development Research Report 2009/53. New York: UNDP.

Korzeniewicz, Roberto, and Timothy Moran, 2009, *Unveiling Inequality: A World-Historical Perspective*. New York: Russell Sage Foundation.

Koser, Khalid, 2007, *International Migration: A Very Short Introduction*. Oxford: Oxford University Press.

* Landau, Loren B., and Aurelia Wa Kabwe Segatti, 2009, *Human Development Impacts of Migration: South Africa Case Study*. Human Development Research Report 2009/05. New York: UNDP.

* Leibbrandt, Murray, et al., 2010, *Trends in South African Income Distribution and Poverty since the Fall of Apartheid*. Cape Town: SALDRU and Paris: OECD.

Manby, Bronwen, 2009, *Struggles for Citizenship in Africa*. London: Zed Books.

* Manby, Bronwen, 2011, *International Law and the Right to Nationality in Sudan*. London: Open Society Foundations.

* Marfouk, Abdeslam, 2007, *African Brain Drain: Scope and Determinants*. Accra: Association of African Universities.

* Martens, Jens, 2010, *Thinking Ahead: Development Models and Indicators of Well-being Beyond the MDGs*. Berlin: Friedrich-Ebert-Stiftung.

* Melonio, Thomas, 2008, *Migration Balances: Concept, Hypotheses and Discussion*. Paris: Agence Française de Développement.

* Mensah, Kwadwo, Maureen Mackintosh, and Leroi Henry, 2005, T*he 'Skills Drain' of Health Professionals from the Developing World*. London: Medact.

* Migrants' Rights Network, 2010, *Migrant Capital: A Perspective on Contemporary Migration in London*. London: Migrants' Rights Network.

* Migration Information Source, 2005, *Migrants' Human Rights: From the Margins to the Mainstream*. Washington, DC: Migration Policy Institute.

Milanovic, Branko, 2007, *Worlds Apart: Measuring International and Global Inequality*. Princeton: Princeton University Press.

* Milanovic, Branko, 2009a, *Global Inequality and the Global Inequality Extraction Ratio: The Story of the Past Two Centuries*. Washington, DC: World Bank.

* Milanovic, Branko, 2009b, *Global Inequality of Opportunity: How Much of Our Income is Determined at Birth?* Washington, DC: World Bank.

Milanovic, Branko, 2011, *The Haves and the Have-Nots*. New York: Basic Books.

* National Network for Immigrant and Refugee Rights, 2010, *Injustice for All: The Rise of the U.S. Immigration Policing Regime*. Oakland, CA: National Network for Immigrant and Refugee Rights.

* Neocosmos, Michael, 2010, *From "Foreign Natives" to "Native Foreigners". Explaining Xenophobia in Post-apartheid South Africa*. 2nd ed. Dakar: Codesria, 2010.

* Ortega, Daniel E., 2009, *Human Development of Peoples*. Human Development Research Paper 2009/49. New York: UNDP.

* Özden, Çağlar and Maurice Schiff (eds.), 2006, *International Migration, Remittances, and the Brain Drain*. Washington, DC: World Bank.

* Pastore, Ferruccio, 2007, *Europe, Migration and Development: Critical remarks on an emerging policy field*. Rome: Centro Studi di Politica Internazionale.

Peberdy, Sally, 2009, *Selecting Immigrants: National Identity and South Africa's Immigration Policies, 1910–2008*. Johannesburg: Wits University Press.

* Pécoud, Antoine, and P. F. A. de Guchteneire, 2005, *Migration without Borders: An Investigation into the Free Movement of People*. Geneva: UNESCO.

Pécoud, Antoine, and P. F. A. de Guchteneire (eds.), 2007, *Migration without Borders: Essays on the Free Movement of People*. Oxford, UK: Berghahn Books.

* Physicians for Human Rights, 2004, *An Action Plan to Prevent Brain Drain: Building Equitable Health Systems in Africa*. Boston: Physicians for Human Rights.

* Polzer, Tara, 2010a, *Population Movements in and to South Africa*. Johannesburg: Forced Migration Studies Program.

* Polzer, Tara, 2010b, *'Xenophobia': Violence against Foreign Nations and other 'Outsiders' in Contemporary South Africa*. Johannesburg: Forced Migration Studies Programme.

* Pritchett, Lant, 2006, *Let Their People Come: Breaking the Gridlock on Global Labor Mobility*. Washington, DC: Center for Global Development.

* Quartey, Peter, 2009, *Migration in Ghana: A Country Profile 2009*. Geneva: International Organization for Migration.

Raissiguier, Catherine, 2010, *Reinventing the Republic: Gender, Migration, and Citizenship in France*. Stanford, CA: Stanford University Press.

* Ratha, Dilip, et al., 2011, *Leveraging Migration for Africa: Remittances, Skills, and Investments*. Washington: World Bank.

Sassen, Saskia, 2006, *Territory, Authority, Rights: From Medieval to Global Assemblages*. Princeton: Princeton University Press.

Shachar, Ayelet, 2009, *The Birthright Lottery: Citizenship and Global Inequality*. Cambridge, MA: Harvard University Press.

* Stiglitz, Joseph E., Sen, Amartya, and Fitoussie, Jean-Paul, 2009, *Report by the Commission on the Measurement of Economic Performance and Social Progress*. Paris: Commission on the Measurement of Economic Performance and Social Progress.

* Strategy and Tactics, 2010, *South African Civil Society and Xenophobia*. Johannesburg: Strategy and Tactics.

* Terrazas, Aaron, 2010, *African Immigrants in the United States*. Washington, DC: Migration Information Source.

* Transatlantic Trends, 2010, *Transatlantic Trends: Immigration*. Washington, DC: Transatlantic Trends.

* UNDP (United Nations Development Program), 2009, *Human Development Report 2009. Overcoming Barriers: Human Mobility and Development*. New York: UNDP.

* UN (United Nations), 2003, *International Convention on the Protection of the Rights of All Migrant Workers and Members of Their Families*. Geneva: United Nations.

* UN (United Nations), 2005, *The International Conventon on Migrant Workers and its Committee: Fact Sheet No. 24 (Rev.1)*. New York and Geneva: United Nations.

* UN (United Nations), 2010, *Human Rights of Migrants* (A/65/222). New York and Geneva: United Nations.

* UNHCR (United Nations High Commission for Refugees), 2008, *Note on International Protection: Report by the High Commissioner (A/AC 96/1053)*. Geneva: UNHCR.

* U.S. Committee for Refugees and Immigrants, 2004, "Warehousing Refugees: A Denial of Rights, A Waste of Humanity," in *World Refugee Survey 2004*. Washington, D.C.: U.S. Committee for Refugees and Immigrants.

Wilkinson, Richard, and Kate Pickett, 2009, *The Spirit Level: Why Greater Equality Makes Societies Stronger*. New York: Bloomsbury Press.

Wilson, Francis, and Mamphela Ramphele, 1989, *Uprooting Poverty: The South African Challenge*. New York: W. W. Norton.

World Bank, 2005, *Global Economic Prospects 2006: Economic Implications of Remittances and Migration*. Washington, DC: World Bank.

World Bank, 2010a, *Outlook for Remittances Flows 2011–2012*. Washington, DC: World Bank.

World Bank, 2010b, *Migration and Remittances Factbook 2011*. Washington, DC: World Bank.

REFERENCES: WEBSITES

AfricaFocus Bulletin migration page
http://www.africafocus.org/migrexp.php

The Age of Migration (companion site to book Castles and Miller, 2009)
http://www.age-of-migration.com

Centre on Migration, Citizenship and Development (COMCAD), University of Bielefeld
http://www.uni-bielefeld.de/tdrc/ag_comcad

Forced Migration Studies Programme, University of the Witwatersrand
http://www.migration.org.za

Global Health Workforce Alliance
http://www.who.int/workforcealliance/en/

Human Development Research Reports for 2009 Report
http://hdr.undp.org/en/reports/global/hdr2009/papers/

International Migration Institute, Oxford University
http://www.imi.ox.ac.uk/

Migrants Rights International
http://www.migrantwatch.org

Migration and Development
http://www.migrationdevelopment.org/

Migration Information Source
http://www.migrationinformation.org/index.cfm

Migration Policy Institute
http://www.migrationpolicy.org/research/migration_development.php

Peoplemove Blog by Dilip Ratha
http://blogs.worldbank.org/peoplemove/

People's Global Action on Migration, Development, and Human Rights.
http://www.mfasia.org/pga/index.html
http://www.accionglobalmexico.org/documentos.php

United Nations High Commissioner for Human Rights
http://www2.ohchr.org/english/issues/migration/

ANNEX: IMPLICATIONS FOR DEVELOPMENT GOALS AND MEASURES

As an illustrative exercise, this annex examines what it might mean if migration were to be taken seriously as showing the need for fundamental changes in common development goals, rather than only a separate unconnected issue. The Millennium Development Goals which now define measures of global progress for 2015 are defined as "anti-poverty" goals[52,] and do not mention inequality. And, with the exception of goal 8, which calls for a vaguely defined "global partnership for development," they all apply only at a national level, and are applied exclusively to developing countries.

Yet the failure to find sustainable solutions to protection of the rights of migrants and the social conflicts related to migration is a constant reminder that global human development does not depend only on developments within individual countries. Relationships between countries, and in particular, the levels of gross inequality that impel high levels of migration, also require measurable goals for progress, even if achievement of those goals faces formidable obstacles.

While these are unlikely to be included in the least common denominator of official consensus, and are undoubtedly more difficult to measure than national-level goals, such a thought experiment should be part of the agenda for expanding the debate. Yet even current efforts to expand the scope of measurements of societal progress fail to consider this transnational dimension.[53]

Such transnational and relational measurements should include measures of transnational inequality, measures for developed countries that might make the concept of "partnership" less vague, and measures for countries of origin, focused on the effectiveness of their policies on emigration and the diaspora.

The most important, and also the most unlikely to be incorporated into official targets, is the level of transnational inequality. At a global scale, notes inequality expert Branko Milanovic (2011: 151–152), global inequality is now at an all-time high of 70 Gini points, greater than in highly unequal countries such as South Africa and Brazil. Although the rising level of aggregate inequality is now being held back by rapid growth in China and India, inequality both between countries and within countries continues to grow. The ratio between the average income of the top 10 percent and the bottom 10 percent is about 80 to 1. According to the 2010 Human Development Report, the average income

---

52. As noted by Milanovic (2011, 84), addressing "poverty," with the aura of charity, is more congenial for the rich than addressing "inequality," which potentially raises the issue of justice.

53. See, above all, the Report by the Commission on the Measurement of Economic Performance and Social Progress (Stiglitz, Sen, and Fitoussi 2009). Other sources include Marten (2010) and the OECD project on "Global Project on Measuring the Progress of Societies" (http://www.wikiprogress.org).

of OECD countries in 2008 ($37,077), was 4.7 times that of the developing Arab states ($7,861) and 18.1 times that of Sub-Saharan Africa ($2,050). Life expectancy of 80.3 years for OECD countries contrasts with 69.1 for developing Arab countries and 52.7 for Sub-Saharan Africa. For mean years of schooling, the comparison is 11.4 to 5.7 and 4.5, respectively.

Such high levels of inequality make continued immigration on a scale far larger than sustainable, with much of it forced by economic need, unavoidable, regardless of the levels of restriction imposed or the attempts at management of migration. Despite rich-country reluctance even to consider setting goals to reduce inequality, that adds a practical incentive to the moral imperative for greater global equality. It also provides a rationale for measuring inequality not only at the global level but within major regional migration systems. Changes in both policies and results will depend on changes in the political and economic power of developing countries themselves, as illustrated in the rising prominence of the BRICS[54] emerging powers. Despite recent increases in growth rates, Africa's bargaining power is much more limited. But it is already time to build a conceptual framework for more ambitious goals, with measurable indicators, that move beyond the Millennium Development Goals.

Hypothetically, if one were to take as a goal "reducing global inequality by half by the year 2050," that could serve as a baseline for similar goals within more limited groups of nations. At a global level, using the Gini index as a measure, that would mean reducing the level of global inequality to 35 Gini points, slightly higher than levels of inequality within most European countries, but lower than that in the United States. Or, taking ratios of average income, this would mean reducing the level of inequality between Europe and Sub-Saharan Africa, for example, to 9 to 1 instead of 18 to 1.

Defining similar measures for groups of related countries could contribute to discussions linking migration issues with those of the related development trajectories of the countries involved. Such measures, for example, would be relevant for evaluating the "Partnership for Democracy and Shared Prosperity with the Southern Mediterranean" announced by the European Union in March 2011. Other sets of regions linked to Africa for which such transnational measures would be relevant include, at the most general level, the OECD countries and Africa, European Union and Africa, North America and Africa, and the non-African Arab world in relation to East, West, and Central Africa. Within Africa, in addition to the levels of inequality within the continent as a whole, the levels of inequality between North Africa and East, West, and Central Africa and those between South Africa and the remainder of Sub-Saharan Africa are both

---

54. Brazil, Russia, India, China, South Africa.

particularly relevant for migration and the equity of development outcomes[55]. In each case, the measure of progress should be demonstrable success in reducing the ratios of inequality between regions at different levels of development.

Focusing on transnational inequality and migration could also facilitate exploring measures of "partnership" which are less vague than those now included in Millennium Development Goal 8. The first target listed for that goal, "develop further an open, rule-based, predictable, non-discriminatory trading and financial system," could, ironically, easily be a prescription for increased inequality. In addition to the familiar indicators already included on aid, market access, and debt sustainability, indicators such as the following could shed light on the realities of partnership:

- Supplement and compare measures of Official Development Assistance with tracking of illicit financial flows from developing to developed countries. The non-governmental organization Global Financial Integrity (http://www.gfip.org) has begun to build the evidence base for such measures, identifying some US$6.5 trillion in such flows out of the developing world from 2000 through 2008 (more than 7 times ODA for the same period). Data on the destination of these flows requires reforms in developed countries on transparency for financial reporting. But judging the net transfer of resources relevant to global inequality is not feasible without their inclusion.
- When estimating the financial effects of migration on origin and destination countries, include not only remittances but also gains and losses due to migration of skilled labor. Using the concept of "migration balances," researcher Thomas Melonio (2008) has proposed such a comparative measure, and suggested that destination countries should assume the obligation (additional to existing levels of development aid) of compensating origin countries for such losses of skilled labor.
- There are elaborate measures of policies for integration of migrants in European and some other developed countries (http://www.mipex.eu). But this should be supplemented by measures that also include the level of openness in relation to the structural demand for migration resulting from transnational inequalities. One such measure, for example, might be the ratio of regular immigrants to the total of irregular immigrants, deportations, and interceptions. Including deportations and interceptions as well as irregular immigrants would ensure that the measure would not be improved by increased restrictions and enhanced enforcement measures that simply displace potential irregular immigrants to other countries.

---

55. Milanovic (2011: 176-186) gives brief summaries of such comparisons within the United States, the European Union, Asia, and Latin America, but not for Africa or regions involved in African migration systems.

For countries of origin of migrants, probably the most relevant measures are simply indicators of whether and how fast they are closing the development gap with potential destination countries for migrants. More specific measures of success, with respect to migration, might include the subjective measure of reducing the number of people who say they want to leave (as measured by the Gallup Potential Net Migration Index, available on http://www.gallup.com) and the more objective measure of reducing the tertiary emigration rate of professionals leaving the country.

In terms of the contribution of the diaspora to development, in addition to the topics of remittances and investments stressed in recent World Bank reports (Ratha et al. 2011), attention could also be given to developing measures of constructive home country to diaspora relationships. This would, of course, require greater efforts to collect data on diaspora populations, including both initiatives by origin countries and collaboration between statistical agencies in origin and destination countries.

The failure of many countries to protect their diasporas has been starkly visible in the crisis of evacuation of migrants from Libya in 2011, as those left behind have been disproportionately those from Sub-Saharan Africa. The extent to which this is a failure only of capacity or also of will is not clear. But it is clear that few African countries have adequate consular facilities to protect their overseas nationals. Significant increases in such efforts would be a highly visible sign of progress, and perhaps even a candidate for indicators such as the ratio of consular officers to diaspora nationals.

Other measures that could be useful should the data be available might include:

- What proportion of emigrants retain citizenship ties to the country of origin? While this would reflect in part the availability of the option of dual citizenship, it would also be an indicator of the extent of loyalty and potential contributions to development in the home country.
- Measures of income and other development indicators for the set of people born in a country, including both residents and emigrants, as suggested by Clemens and Pritchett (2008). In terms of measuring human development, this would give equal weight to people born in a country, whether they move or stay.
- An appropriate complement to such a measure would be the levels of inequality between those in the diaspora and home-country residents. The greater the gap, the less likely that relationships with the diaspora would or should be viewed as sustainable contributions to national development.

CURRENT AFRICAN ISSUES PUBLISHED BY THE INSTITUTE

Recent issues in the series are available electronically
for download free of charge www.nai.uu.se

1. *South Africa, the West and the Frontline States. Report from a Seminar.* 1981, 34 pp, (out-of print)
2. Maja Naur, *Social and Organisational Change in Libya.* 1982, 33 pp, (out-of print)
3. *Peasants and Agricultural Production in Africa. A Nordic Research Seminar. Follow-up Reports and Discussions.* 1981, 34 pp, (out-of print)
4. Ray Bush & S. Kibble, *Destabilisation in Southern Africa, an Overview.* 1985, 48 pp, (out-of print)
5. Bertil Egerö, *Mozambique and the Southern African Struggle for Liberation.* 1985, 29 pp, (out-of print)
6. Carol B.Thompson, *Regional Economic Polic under Crisis Condition. Southern African Development.* 1986, 34 pp, (out-of print)
7. Inge Tvedten, *The War in Angola, Internal Conditions for Peace and Recovery.* 1989, 14 pp, (out-of print)
8. Patrick Wilmot, *Nigeria's Southern Africa Policy 1960–1988.* 1989, 15 pp, (out-of print)
9. Jonathan Baker, *Perestroika for Ethiopia: In Search of the End of the Rainbow?* 1990, 21 pp, (out-of print)
10. Horace Campbell, *The Siege of Cuito Cuanavale.* 1990, 35 pp, (out-of print)
11. Maria Bongartz, *The Civil War in Somalia. Its genesis and dynamics.* 1991, 26 pp, (out-of print)
12. Shadrack B.O. Gutto, *Human and People's Rights in Africa. Myths, Realities and Prospects.* 1991, 26 pp, (out-of print)
13. Said Chikhi, *Algeria. From Mass Rebellion to Workers' Protest.* 1991, 23 pp, (out-of print)
14. Bertil Odén, *Namibia's Economic Links to South Africa.* 1991, 43 pp, (out-of print)
15. Cervenka Zdenek, *African National Congress Meets Eastern Europe. A Dialogue on Common Experiences.* 1992, 49 pp, ISBN 91-7106-337-4, (out-of print)
16. Diallo Garba, *Mauritania–The Other Apartheid?* 1993, 75 pp, ISBN 91-7106-339-0, (out-of print)
17. Zdenek Cervenka and Colin Legum, *Can National Dialogue Break the Power of Terror in Burundi?* 1994, 30 pp, ISBN 91-7106-353-6, (out-of print)
18. Erik Nordberg and Uno Winblad, *Urban Environmental Health and Hygiene in Sub-Saharan Africa.* 1994, 26 pp, ISBN 91-7106-364-1, (out-of print)
19. Chris Dunton and Mai Palmberg, *Human Rights and Homosexuality in Southern Africa.* 1996, 48 pp, ISBN 91-7106-402-8, (out-of print)
20. Georges Nzongola-Ntalaja *From Zaire to the Democratic Republic of the Congo.* 1998, 18 pp, ISBN 91-7106-424-9, (out-of print)
21. Filip Reyntjens, *Talking or Fighting? Political Evolution in Rwanda and Burundi, 1998–1999.* 1999, 27 pp, ISBN 91-7106-454-0, SEK 80.-
22. Herbert Weiss, *War and Peace in the Democratic Republic of the Congo.* 1999, 28 pp, ISBN 91-7106-458-3, SEK 80,-
23. Filip Reyntjens, *Small States in an Unstable Region – Rwanda and Burundi, 1999–2000,* 2000, 24 pp, ISBN 91-7106-463-X, (out-of print)
24. Filip Reyntjens, *Again at the Crossroads: Rwanda and Burundi, 2000–2001.* 2001, 25 pp, ISBN 91-7106-483-4, (out-of print)
25. Henning Melber, *The New African Initiative and the African Union. A Preliminary Assessment and Documentation.* 2001, 36 pp, ISBN 91-7106-486-9, (out-of print)

26. Dahilon Yassin Mohamoda, *Nile Basin Cooperation. A Review of the Literature.* 2003, 39 pp, ISBN 91-7106-512-1, SEK 90,-
27. Henning Melber (ed.), *Media, Public Discourse and Political Contestation in Zimbabwe.* 2004, 39 pp, ISBN 91-7106-534-2, SEK 90,-
28. Georges Nzongola-Ntalaja, *From Zaire to the Democratic Republic of the Congo.* Second and Revised Edition. 2004, 23 pp, ISBN-91-7106-538-5, (out-of print)
29. Henning Melber (ed.), *Trade, Development, Cooperation – What Future for Africa?* 2005, 44 pp, ISBN 91-7106-544-X, SEK 90,-
30. Kaniye S.A. Ebeku, *The Succession of Faure Gnassingbe to the Togolese Presidency – An International Law Perspective.* 2005, 32 pp, ISBN 91-7106-554-7, SEK 90,-
31. Jeffrey V. Lazarus, Catrine Christiansen, Lise Rosendal Østergaard, Lisa Ann Richey, *Models for Life – Advancing antiretroviral therapy in sub-Saharan Africa.* 2005, 33 pp, ISBN 91-7106-556-3, SEK 90,-
32. Charles Manga Fombad and Zein Kebonang, *AU, NEPAD and the APRM – Democratisation Efforts Explored.* Edited by Henning Melber. 2006, 56 pp, ISBN 91-7106-569-5, SEK 90,-
33. Pedro Pinto Leite, Claes Olsson, Magnus Schöldtz, Toby Shelley, Pål Wrange, Hans Corell and Karin Scheele, *The Western Sahara Conflict – The Role of Natural Resources in Decolonization.* Edited by Claes Olsson. 2006, 32 pp, ISBN 91-7106-571-7, SEK 90,-
34. Jassey, Katja and Stella Nyanzi, *How to Be a "Proper" Woman in the Times of HIV and AIDS.* 2007, 35 pp, ISBN 91-7106-574-1, SEK 90,-
35. Lee, Margaret, Henning Melber, Sanusha Naidu and Ian Taylor, *China in Africa.* Compiled by Henning Melber. 2007, 47 pp, ISBN 978-91-7106-589-6, SEK 90,-
36. Nathaniel King, *Conflict as Integration. Youth Aspiration to Personhood in the Teleology of Sierra Leone's 'Senseless War'.* 2007, 32 pp, ISBN 978-91-7106-604-6, SEK 90,-
37. Aderanti Adepoju, *Migration in sub-Saharan Africa.* 2008. 70 pp, ISBN 978-91-7106-620-6, SEK 110,-
38. Bo Malmberg, *Demography and the development potential of sub-Saharan Africa.* 2008, 39 pp, 978-91-7106-621-3
39. Johan Holmberg, *Natural resources in sub-Saharan Africa: Assets and vulnerabilities.* 2008, 52 pp, 978-91-7106-624-4
40. Arne Bigsten and Dick Durevall, *The African economy and its role in the world economy.* 2008, 66 pp, 978-91-7106-625-1
41. Fantu Cheru, *Africa's development in the 21st century: Reshaping the research agenda.* 2008, 47 pp, 978-91-7106-628-2
42. Dan Kuwali, *Persuasive Prevention. Towards a Principle for Implementing Article 4(h) and R2P by the African Union.* 2009. 70 pp. ISBN 978-91-7106-650-3
43. Daniel Volman, *China, India, Russia and the United States. The Scramble for African Oil and the Militarization of the Continent.* 2009. 24 pp. ISBN 978-91-7106-658-9
44. Mats Hårsmar, *Understanding Poverty in Africa? A Navigation through Disputed Concepts, Data and Terrains.* 2010. 54 pp. ISBN 978-91-7106-668-8
45. Sam Maghimbi, Razack B. Lokina and Mathew A. Senga, *The Agrarian Question in Tanzania? A State of the Art Paper.* 2011. 67 pp. ISBN 978-91-7106-684-8
46. William Minter, *African Migration, Global Inequalities, and Human Rights. Connecting the Dots.* 2011. 95 pp. ISBN 978-91-7106-692-3

www.ingramcontent.com/pod-product-compliance
Ingram Content Group UK Ltd.
Pitfield, Milton Keynes, MK11 3LW, UK
UKHW051652180426
11947UKWH00021B/1915